About Demos

Who we are
Demos is the think tank for everyday democracy. We believe everyone should be able to make personal choices in their daily lives that contribute to the common good. Our aim is to put this democratic idea into practice by working with organisations in ways that make them more effective and legitimate.

What we work on
We focus on six areas: public services; science and technology; cities and public space; people and communities; arts and culture; and global security.

Who we work with
Our partners include policy-makers, companies, public service providers and social entrepreneurs. Demos is not linked to any party but we work with politicians across political divides. Our international network – which extends across Eastern Europe, Scandinavia, Australia, Brazil, India and China – provides a global perspective and enables us to work across borders.

How we work
Demos knows the importance of learning from experience. We test and improve our ideas in practice by working with people who can make change happen. Our collaborative approach means that our partners share in the creation and ownership of new ideas.

What we offer
We analyse social and political change, which we connect to innovation and learning in organisations. We help our partners show thought leadership and respond to emerging policy challenges.

How we communicate
As an independent voice, we can create debates that lead to real change. We use the media, public events, workshops and publications to communicate our ideas. All our books can be downloaded free from the Demos website.

www.demos.co.uk

First published in 2006
© Demos
Some rights reserved – see copyright licence for details

ISBN 1 84180 169 0
Copy edited by Julie Pickard, London
Typeset by utimestwo, Collingtree, Northants
Printed by Iprint, Leicester

For further information and
subscription details please contact:

Demos
Magdalen House
136 Tooley Street
London SE1 2TU

telephone: 0845 458 5949
email: hello@demos.co.uk
web: www.demos.co.uk

Bringing it Home
Community-based approaches
to counter-terrorism

Rachel Briggs
Catherine Fieschi
Hannah Lownsbrough

DEM⊙S

DEM⊙S

Contents

Acknowledgements

We have benefited enormously from the support and guidance of so many people. There are too many to name them all individually, but we should say special thanks to a number who have made important contributions to this piece of research.

First, thanks to our steering group: Faye Auty, Abdul Haqq Baker, Rob Beckley, Stuart Croft, Thelma Gillen, Phil Gormley, Phoebe Griffith, Michael Hallowes, Robin Hart, Hisham Hellyer, Dilwar Hussain, Huda Jawad, Sadiq Khan MP, Bob Lambert, Sally Leivesley, Tony Lord, Emran Mian, Gavin Proudley, Dave Tucker and Keith Weston.

Second, thanks to the organisations whose generous support made this piece of research possible: the Association of Chief Police Officers (ACPO), the Arts and Humanities Research Council (AHRC), the Economic and Social Research Council (ESRC) and the Cohesion and Faiths Unit at the Department for Communities and Local Government (DCLG), which was formerly based at the Home Office.

Third, special thanks to a number of people who made important contributions along the way: Tahir Abbas, Musa Abubaker Admani, Khurshid Ahmed, Sughra Ahmed, Azad Ali, Rushanara Ali, AbdurRahmaan Anderson, Yahya Birt, Joanne Brooks, Tufyal Choudrey, John Denham, Shareefa Fulat, Frank Gardner, Mohamed Mukadam, Cosh Omar, Hasan Patel, Tariq Ramadan, Nasreen Suleaman and Salma Yaqoob.

Finally, a big thank you to all our colleagues at Demos who have offered insight and support at key moments during the project, but especially to Virna Di Palma, Mark Fuller, Lisa Ginsborg, Olga Gora, Sian Jones and Simon Stephens.

As ever, all mistakes and omissions remain our own.

Rachel Briggs
Catherine Fieschi
Hannah Lownsbrough
December 2006

Methodology

This report is the result of a year-long research project supported by financial contributions from the Cohesion and Faiths Unit at the Department for Communities and Local Government (DCLG), which was formerly based at the Home Office, the Association of Chief Police Officers (ACPO), the Economic and Social Research Council (ESRC) and the Arts and Humanities Research Council (AHRC).

Researchers carried out an initial stage of background research, drawing on existing academic and policy work, demographic data, policy documents and initial interviews with members of the Muslim community. The methodology, approach and tentative conclusions were tested extensively at a Demos conference at Wilton Park in March 2006, which brought together senior police and security service personnel, Whitehall-based civil servants, community activists, academics and journalists. The conference tested the hypothesis that community-based approaches to counter-terrorism are effective and provided invaluable feedback and suggestions for further research.

Researchers then undertook interviews, group discussions and informal conversations in a number of cities around the UK, including Birmingham, Leeds, Leicester and London. This element of the research was critical, as so much of this kind of research tends to be London-centric. During the course of the fieldwork, researchers talked to well over 200 people, most of whom were residents of Muslim communities – school children, university students, parents, community leaders, religious leaders, and so forth – but also included local police officers, local authority officials, politicians, journalists and academics.

The majority of these interviews were conducted strictly off the record because of the potential sensitivities around some of the issues covered, and for this reason many of the quotes in the report are unattributed. This was essential in enabling individuals to be more open in their comments than might otherwise have been the case.

Researchers also benefited from help and advice throughout from the project steering group, which included academics, community activists, politicians and NGO staff. A full list of the steering group is included in the Acknowledgements.

1. Introduction

The current threat from Islamist terrorism is serious and sustained. It is genuinely international in scope, involving a variety of groups, networks and individuals driven by particular violent and extremist beliefs. It is indiscriminate – aiming to cause mass casualties, regardless of the age, nationality, or religion of their victims; and the terrorists are often prepared to commit suicide to kill others. Overall, we judge that the scale of the threat is potentially still increasing and is not likely to diminish significantly for some years.[1]

At 8.50am on 7 July 2005, al Qaida finally came home to roost. The group had been building its base in the UK for 15 years; in the 1990s London was one of its main global hubs, evidenced by the fact that between 1996 and 1998 nearly one-fifth of the calls from Osama bin Laden's mobile phone were to hardwired and mobile phones in the UK.[2] The country also became an important spiritual centre for the group, home to three radical Islamist clerics, Omar Bakri Muhammed, Omar Mahmud Otham (Abu Qatada) and Moustafa Kamel (Abu Hamza). This earned the capital the title 'Londonistan' by commentator Melanie Phillips who, along with others such as Michael Gove, has accused the government of pursuing a policy of active appeasement, which enabled al Qaida to put down such strong roots here. As long as they didn't attack the UK, they were welcome to stay.

Everything changed on 11 September 2001, when al Qaida launched an attack of cinematic proportions. Overnight, the world sat up and took notice of Osama bin Laden, who for years had been more a figure of fun than one of fear for intelligence agencies around the world. As images of the collapsing World Trade Center towers dominated television screens and newspaper front pages for months, the vision of al Qaida was fixed in all of our minds: a global terror network with international ambitions that would stop at nothing to deliver death and destruction to the West. Osama bin Laden, commander-in-chief, pulling the levers from a cave in Afghanistan, was cast into the role of international bogeyman, his personification of everything antithetical to western values – premodern, deeply religious, self-sacrifice for the cause – playing directly into the fears and anxieties of the West.

The UK government's response was proportionate: big, bold, symbolic and global. There have been posturing, chest-beating speeches to world leaders, initiatives through the G8, partnerships with European allies, a raft of new legislation, and wars in Afghanistan and Iraq. It has also tightened the screw on al Qaida's network in the UK, proscribing a number of organisations and cracking down on the so-called preachers of hate, such as Abu Hamza, who is now languishing in jail.

Then, almost four years on from September 11, Britain experienced its own al Qaida attack. The government, police and Security Service had told us to expect it, but when it eventually came, those reminders did nothing to lessen the blow. Perhaps if, like September 11 and Madrid, it had been carried out by foreigners, it might have been easier to take in. But the fact that it was perpetrated by four ordinary, British lads, from respectable families, who passed the Norman Tebbitt cricket test with flying colours, made it harder to comprehend and left us uncertain about how to react. The government's fear of home-grown terrorism had finally been realised.

Hindsight is a wonderful luxury in which this report does not wish to indulge. The threat we face today is serious and sustained, and we must therefore concentrate on tackling it, rather than playing cheap games of political 'told you so'. However, it is worth dwelling on two strategic errors that our politicians and security experts made on 11 September, which have hindered our responses ever since and, in some cases, made them counterproductive. These are both lessons we need to learn if we are to move forward.

First, the magnitude of September 11 and the audacity of Osama bin Laden made us lose sight of the fact that terrorism is a social and political phenomenon that needs local roots to take hold. The international network and the concept of the 'umma' – the global community of which every Muslim is a part – are important features of al Qaida, but distant and global concerns can gain currency only when they are able to feed off local, everyday, personal grievances, such as those experienced by Muslims in the UK. Our Muslim communities suffer some of the worst indicators of deprivation, discrimination and social exclusion, and many are deeply unhappy about aspects of the government's foreign policy towards the Islamic world, which they feel constitutes a 'war on Islam'. Cheap international travel, satellite television and continuing links to family and friends in countries of origin provide a vital bridge between these personal and global grievances.

When you are caught in the headlights, all oncoming vehicles tend to look like juggernauts, and after September 11, our politicians and security forces were too quick to focus on al Qaida's global credentials. In the five years since September 11, there has been very little consideration of the local dynamic or the value that Muslim communities could add to counter-terrorism efforts.

Second, the almost exclusive focus on the group – its membership, infrastructure and modus operandi – distracted politicians and security forces from the fact that terrorists prefer to get other people to do their work for them. Too often, the things we do in the name of 'security' alienate the very people we need to engage. David Fromkin's words from over 30 years ago are just as valid today:

> *Terrorism is violence used in order to create fear; but it is aimed at creating fear in order that the fear, in turn, will lead*

> *somebody else – not the terrorist – to embark on some quite*
> *different program of action that will accomplish whatever it is*
> *that the terrorist really desires.*[3]

In other words, when a terrorist kills, the goal is not murder itself but
something else, such as a police crackdown, that will create a rift
between government and society that the terrorist can then exploit
for revolutionary purpose.[4] *Bringing it Home* shows that the
government's response to terrorism is alienating the very
communities it needs to engage, and that their growing sense of
grievance, anger and injustice inadvertently legitimises the terrorists'
aims, with or without their active consent.

The London bombings highlighted the importance of community
engagement and the government responded accordingly. Less than
two weeks after the attack, the Prime Minister had gathered Muslim
leaders into Downing Street, and soon after the Home Office had
launched its Preventing Extremism Together (PET) initiative to work
with the community on ways to combat extremism and its causes. But
over a year on, the prognosis is not good. The government's attempts
to engage Muslims in the policy-making process have been criticised
as being rushed, conducted on the government's terms, failing to
break away from the usual suspects, and with little follow through.
The government has also been highly reluctant to engage with the
many reasonable grievances of the community – from Iraq to social
justice – in the fear that any kind of acknowledgement could suggest
that the terrorists have just cause or that the government is somehow
complicit. This has made honest conversations difficult, as too many
vital subjects remain out of bounds.

These initiatives also took place against a backdrop of conflicting
government messages. In the meeting rooms of Whitehall, ministers
were assuring Muslim leaders of the need for partnership, but in press
briefings they were talking of the need for Muslims to 'get serious'
about terrorism, spy on their children, and put up with inconveniences in the greater good of national security. And a number
of counter-terrorist interventions, most notably Forest Gate, have

illustrated a reluctance to operationalise the concept of community engagement in practice.

Bringing it Home argues that we need to put communities at the heart of our approaches to counter-terrorism for four reasons. First, they offer important sources of information and intelligence: our own in-built early warning system. This is especially important against a group such as al Qaida, which is willing to inflict mass carnage with no warning whatsoever. Second, communities picking up these signs are best placed to act pre-emptively to divert their young people from extremism: the self-policing society. Third, while the state must also play a role, communities must take the lead in tackling problems that either create grievances or hinder their ability to organise, such as poverty, poor educational and employment attainment, and the paucity of effective leadership and representation. Finally, the police and Security Service cannot act without the consent of the communities they are there to protect. There are those who would argue that Muslims should tolerate inconveniences for the greater good, effectively put up and shut up. But this illustrates a lack of understanding about how security is really delivered in practice – always through consent, never through force. The nature of the threat from al Qaida means that the police will often need to intervene much earlier, thereby increasing the risks that they will make mistakes. Sustaining this practice over the long term will be possible only if the police secure the active consent of the Muslim community, which will need to give them the benefit of the doubt on such occasions.

A community-based approach to counter-terrorism must be underpinned by four principles. First, it must be locally based and recognise and respond to the differences within the Muslim community, which is far from homogenous. Second, it needs to be rooted in an understanding of faith, without which it is easy for government and security forces to misread the signs within the community. Third, the government must make the policy-making process as transparent and accountable as possible, opening up decision-making processes and engaging on issues where there is political discontent. Only then will trust be forged between the government and Muslim communities. Fourth, and related, the government must get over its hang-ups about responding to the grievances of the Muslim community. In many instances, they are well founded and deserve to be recognised, but in others the government must be more confident about taking the debate out to the communities, rather than sulking in Whitehall.

Bringing it Home sets out a six-pronged strategy for a community-based approach to counter-terrorism, which spans social justice, community cohesion and counter-terrorism. The breadth of the strategy is important in reducing the inconsistencies between different approaches across government and security forces. The conclusion provides greater detail, but in short, the strategy aims to:

- enhance the lives of Muslims by tackling poverty, low attainment and discrimination
- strengthen community infrastructure
- improve leadership, both by the government and within the Muslim community
- open up the foreign policy-making process to greater scrutiny and provide opportunity for input from all parts of British communities
- divert youth from extremism
- put communities at the heart of counter-terrorist intervention and policing, as an integrated part rather than an add-on or an afterthought.

Perhaps one of the most important factors that could limit the successful implementation of a community-based approach to counter-terrorism is the emergence of a lazy parlance in which the words 'violent extremist' and 'radical' have become interchangeable. Any community that feels deprived, victimised or threatened will produce members who express their frustrations in a variety of ways. Some will look for positions of power to address injustices through official channels; some will stand back in apathy or through a sense of powerlessness; and others will take to the streets in vocal protest. Sometimes – but not always – a small minority will resort to violence, from riots and street fighting to terrorism and armed insurgency. In the current climate, any Muslim expressing anything other than unremitting support for the government is under suspicion, as if there were a slippery slope from anger to frustration to protest and finally violence. Not only does this close down the space for important debates about issues which are causing understandable frustration, but it also limits the parts of the Muslim community with which the government can engage.

That is not to say that there is a clear line to be drawn between violent extremists and radicals. The former are always radicals, but radicals are very rarely violent, and because the government has a fairly poor understanding of the complexities within the community, it often finds it difficult tell them apart. Certain kinds of behaviour, dress and attitudes – for instance among the Salafi community – are problematic for a secular, liberal state such as the UK, and raise wider questions about the status of faith in British politics, the legitimacy or otherwise of certain forms of sharia law, and an individual's right to behave in the private realm in ways that might be at odds with social norms or even laws. These are important questions that we need to debate as a society, but we must not let them get in the way of the priority of tackling terrorism. The energy of these non-violent forms of mobilisation must be harnessed towards this shared goal.

There are no easy options, no quick fixes and no risk-free strategies against the threat of terror posed by al Qaida. It is a particularly challenging foe, which requires us to move seamlessly between the local and the global in our response and maintain a delicate balance between operational interventions and long-term relationship-building. We are also dealing with a community that is feeling more and more alienated and fragile, which is fast closing in on itself, and which has been badly bruised by government efforts at engagement.

However, all our experience in Northern Ireland taught us that the 'hardware' is useless without the 'software'. It was only once we realised that, far from being a distraction to counter-terrorism activities, communities were in fact central to their success, that we finally saw light at the end of the tunnel. The global dimensions, ambitions and rhetoric of al Qaida distracted us from the truth about terrorism, and it is now time to refocus. While this report paints a bleak picture of what has been done in recent years, it is essentially an optimistic volume. *Bringing it Home* argues that it is not too late to operationalise a community-based approach to counter-terrorism, but warns that the window of opportunity is narrowing. If we can make it work now, we will finally be able to start fighting this 'war on terror' on our terms rather than theirs.

2. The problem with the official response so far

On the morning of 7 July 2005 the British heart skipped a beat. The government, police and Security Service had been warning for some time that it was a question of 'when', not 'if', but reminders of those warnings did nothing to lessen the blow: 52 people were killed and hundreds more were seriously injured on their way to work by four young British men, born and raised here, who were willing to blow themselves up in the process. The shock and loss seemed all the greater because of our uncertainty as to how to react. We were left feeling vulnerable and unprepared – and perhaps even slightly complicit in their crime.

Six months after the London bombings, the Commissioner of the Metropolitan Police, Sir Ian Blair, admitted that things were getting worse rather than better and that his force was spending 75 per cent more time on counter-terrorism operations since the London bombings. In an interview with the *Guardian*, he said:

> *The level of threat has intensified and continues to intensify. The terrorists are here and they are going to go on attempting to kill people like you and people like me. The sky is dark . . . there are currently people in the UK as we speak who are planning mass atrocities and who will use suicide as a weapon.*[5]

In a Demos lecture less than 24 hours before the raids and arrests of 10 August 2006, Home Secretary John Reid said: 'We are probably in the most sustained period of severe threat since the end of World War II.'[6]

The threat is indeed serious and real, but our understanding of it remains partial. While 11 September 2001 threw al Qaida into the western consciousness, al Qaida had been growing since the early 1990s. During those intervening years, the response of the government and security agencies has lurched from indifference to appeasement, from hard-fisted tactics to community engagement, depending not just on the nature of the threat assessments, but also on competing agendas, and the political and media climate.

Despite this long run in and the UK's experience of domestic terrorism in Northern Ireland, the government was caught off guard by the London bombings; it was only after an al Qaida attack at home that there was a serious recognition of the importance of community engagement in counter-terrorism. But the government's ability today to get the Muslim community on board is hampered by its historical 'yo-yoing' on the issue and the ongoing lack of consistency between different government departments and between the government and security forces of the state. This has – rightly or wrongly – created an aura of insincerity around these initiatives.

To understand both the threat and the inconsistency of the response to this threat, it is important to have a clear picture of the evolution of al Qaida in Europe.

The Bosnian connection

The origins of al Qaida can be traced as far back as the Afghan–Soviet war, but the genesis of al Qaida in Europe is most directly linked to the conflict in Bosnia in the early 1990s. Bosnia was a stepping stone towards western Europe for Osama bin Laden; it offered a place to train, coalesce into cells and seek shelter from prosecution by foreign law enforcement, in proximity of London, Riyadh and Cairo. It stirred the imagination of a new generation of young Muslims across Europe as it became part legend, part sob-story: a propaganda tale as well as an open wound demanding vengeance. It attracted a number of European Muslims who later returned home converted to the cause, with rudimentary training in warfare and contacts in the Middle East, Africa and Asia.[7] Those who fought there have become the stuff of legend. As Abu Uthman al-Kuwaiti, a senior Afghan–Bosnian veteran, said:

> Those brothers, they were united. But they had not been united on nationalism, neither were they united on socialism, nor were they united by a common tongue. But they were joined together by tawheed [religious unity] and their obedience and devotion to Allah. It can truly be said that these brothers of ours are the cream of society. By Allah, we have not seen men such as these before![8]

During our research, a number of imams from mosques and universities reported seeing signs of radicalisation emerging from the early 1990s onwards, which could be linked to the activity in Bosnia. One told us: 'We started getting concerned as far back as the early 1990s when some individuals started to talk about jihad and the global struggle.' At the time, intelligence agencies failed to see the significance of these events. The rise of al Qaida coincided with the end of the Cold War when local issues were taking precedence. An anonymous Spanish security official admitted to *Time* magazine reporters:

> In Europe we were too preoccupied with our own terrorist problems – ETA in Spain, the IRA in the UK, the Corsicans in France and so on – and we devoted our resources to these threats. . . . Even after the attacks on the US embassies in Kenya and Tanzania, the Islamic threat seemed distant. Everything changed after Sept. 11. Before then we looked on Bin Laden as someone from another planet, like a Martian.[9]

Londonistan?

During the 1990s, London became one of the most important global hubs for al Qaida activity.[10] Analysis of Osama bin Laden's mobile phone billing records between 1996 and 1998 revealed that nearly one-fifth of his calls were made to hardwired and mobile phones in the UK, and al Qaida's Advice and Reformation Committee (ARC) office in Beethoven Street, West Kilburn, was the perfect cover for Osama bin Laden's activities. London was also al Qaida's spiritual hub in the western world. Three radical Islamist clerics were based in Britain during this period – Omar Bakri Muhammed, Omar Mahmud Otham (Abu Qatada) and Moustafa Kamel (Abu Hamza). Some of those who listened to their sermons went on to play an active role within al Qaida, most notoriously Richard Reid (the so-called 'shoe bomber') and Zacarias Moussaoui (the 'twentieth hijacker').

Respected security experts, such as Rohan Gunaratna, claim that 'turning a blind eye' became official government policy during this period. He argues that the UK government allowed radical Muslim groups that incited violence to stay in the UK as long as they did not attack the UK. The British government, he claims, woke up to the limitations of this approach in 2002 and outlawed 21 organisations, 16 of which were Muslim. One French defence ministry official said:

> It may not be the moment to say it, but London is paying for its mistakes, for allowing all those radical organisations from Saudis to Pakistanis to set up shop in London, put out newsletters, make recruits and gather funds to finance their activities.[11]

Commentators such as Melanie Phillips[12] and Michael Gove[13] argue that the UK government continues to pursue a policy of appeasement with Islamist extremists, which creates yet more fundamentalist terror.

There is certainly a grain of truth in Phillips' 'Londonistan' thesis. However, she perhaps gives the government too much credit. In many cases, the government's actions can be explained by a lack of knowledge rather than shrewd political judgement. The Security Service and police were unsure about the nature of the threat we faced and alarm bells were not sounded after the first attempt to blow up the World Trade Center in 1993 nor after the bombings of the US embassies in Africa in 1998, nor in response to the attack on the USS Cole. When the West finally took notice on 11 September 2001, it was too late: al Qaida was already firmly embedded in Europe.

The response to September 11 was the launch of a global 'war on terror' and the invasion of a Muslim country just a month later. It played directly into the hands of al Qaida and its propaganda machine. Suddenly, its offer to Middle Eastern youth also had appeal to Muslims in the West who were able to project their own personal and local grievances onto the al Qaida narrative of Muslim persecution and retribution against the West. Some of the Muslims we spoke to described their fear in the days and weeks following the attacks, when they were extremely worried that they might have to leave the UK because of increased Islamophobia. One woman said: 'We started to talk about where we would go if things got too bad, but we don't really have anywhere to go back to. Those were dark days.'

The growing threat within the UK

Home Secretary John Reid's rhetoric may often seem controversial, but his assessment of the threat we face from home-grown terrorism is accurate: the threat is real and it is acute. As a July 2006 paper on the UK government's counter-terrorism strategy said:

> The current threat from Islamist terrorism is serious and sustained. It is genuinely international in scope, involving a variety of groups, networks and individuals driven by particular violent and extremist beliefs. It is indiscriminate – aiming to cause mass casualties, regardless of the age, nationality, or religion of their victims; and the terrorists are often prepared to commit suicide to kill others. Overall, we judge that the scale of the threat is potentially still increasing and is not likely to diminish significantly for some years.[14]

Nobody knows the exact number of actual and potential activists in the UK, but 200 people are thought to have returned from training camps in Afghanistan, Chechnya or Bosnia; up to 100 Muslim men are thought to have left Britain to fight against coalition troops in Iraq, with at least three killed in combat; and the names of 1200 British citizens (who had trained with al Qaida) were found in a cave in Tora Bora, Afghanistan. In a rare public lecture on 10 November 2006, Dame Eliza Manningham-Buller, Director-General of the Security Service, said:

> *My officers and the police are working to contend with some 200 groupings or networks, totalling over 1600 identified individuals (and there will be many we don't know) who are actively engaged in plotting, or facilitating, terrorist acts here and overseas.*[15]

She went on to say that her service is aware of, and dealing with, around 30 known plots in the UK to kill people and damage the economy.

The importance of community-based approaches

The government's current strategy for tackling terrorism is known as CONTEST. Created in early 2003 but made public only in 2006, it is based on four 'P's which span all aspects of the counter-terrorism agenda: PREVENTING terrorism by tackling the radicalisation of individuals; PURSUING terrorists and those that sponsor them; PROTECTING the public, key national services, and UK interests overseas; and PREPARING for the consequences.[16]

Before 7 July 2005, prevention – the so-called 'softer' end of the strategy – did not receive adequate attention or resources. An April 2005 report from the House of Commons Home Affairs Select Committee, 'Terrorism and Community Relations', criticised the government for putting too much emphasis on the other parts of the strategy at the expense of prevention: 'It is not clear that there is a coherent strategy, developed with the Muslim community, for tackling extremism.'[17] The committee called for an explicit, broader counter-terrorism strategy consisting of more than just a 'set of police and judicial powers'. It concluded: 'In the context of international terrorism, it must explicitly and specifically set out how British Muslim leaders will be supported in assisting British Muslims in resisting extremist views.'[18] A member of the committee complained that the government still does not have a handle on the background causes, and that too much time and money continue to be focused on the 'harder' end of the counter-terrorism spectrum.

Community engagement is often dealt with as if it is separate from – at times even at odds with – mainstream counter-terrorism work, meaning that relationships, principles and lessons are swept aside as operational imperatives take precedence. It is still perceived as a standalone activity carried out by 'community and diversity' types, while the 'real action' remains the preserve of secret police and intelligence officers. And yet, all of our experience in Northern Ireland told us that community engagement is the cornerstone of effective counter-terrorism policy, influencing both the formation and implementation of policy.

Engaging communities in policy-making

In the aftermath of 7 July 2005, the government launched the 'Preventing Extremism Together' (PET) initiative in an attempt to work in partnership with Muslim communities to fight the threat from home-grown terrorism. Home Office ministers visited nine towns and cities with large Muslim populations and held consultations with over a thousand British Muslims to discuss ways in which the government could work with communities to prevent extremism. Subsequently, seven working groups were established to examine priority areas defined by the Home Office, and the exercise produced 64 recommendations, 27 for the government and 37 for Muslim communities. The working groups were asked to consider engaging with young people, education, Muslim women, supporting regional and local initiatives and community actions, imam training and accreditation and the role of mosques as a resource for the whole community, community security, and tackling extremism and radicalisation.

The events of 7 July 2005 provided the impetus for action and change. Muslim leaders who had previously been critical of the government's approach – especially over Iraq and foreign policy – put their disagreements to one side in order to work together to tackle the problems facing their community and the UK as a whole. But more than a year on, the prognosis is not good. At best, PET seems to have been a wasted opportunity. Our research suggests that, rather than building bridges between the government and community, it has made them worse.

Missed opportunities: how government got it wrong

A number of criticisms have been levelled at the Home Office. First, the initiative was rushed. It began just over a month after the 7 July attack and many agreed with the need to seize the moment, but it was completed in little more than three months, which many have argued was unrealistic. Home-grown terrorism is a complex problem that requires considerable time and space to tackle effectively; a series of roundtables with a handful of people thrown together largely because of their proximity to the Home Office was always unlikely to produce lasting solutions.

Second, the schedule was problematic. The process coincided with Ramadan, the Islamic holy period when Muslims fast during daylight hours. Arranging a meeting at such an important point in the religious calendar was perhaps unavoidable. But when this decision was judged against a catalogue of other cultural and religious insensitivities it was taken to betray a telling lack of religious and cultural knowledge on the part of civil servants, thereby reducing their credibility in the eyes of many participants. One working group member told us:

> I didn't expect them [civil servants] to have an intimate knowledge of Islam, but when I received an invitation at short notice to a meeting on Eid . . . I thought it showed there wasn't even a basic knowledge. This didn't inspire confidence in their ability to handle such a complex and sensitive issue.

Third, there are serious questions about the extent to which those Muslims engaged were qualified to represent their communities. A glance around the table at the initial meeting at Downing Street on 19 July 2005 was illuminating – there were no women present and very few people under the age of 50. In short, the government was talking to the usual suspects, although the working groups and discussions around the country did achieve a better balance. Andy Hull of the Metropolitan Police Authority said:

Officials always complain about how difficult it is to reach the 'hard to reach', but rarely have proactive strategies been put in place to build these relationships. In my experience, it is not impossible to get young people along to meetings, but you have to take time to build their trust and ensure that the meetings are conducted on their terms, rather than ours.[19]

The government has also been cautious about being seen to be close to those groups that might have some understanding of al Qaida, fearful of the types of attacks mounted by commentators such as Melanie Phillips. These are groups that are radical and fundamental in their outlook (but not violent), whose religious roots are closest to those of al Qaida, and who therefore tend to come across recruiters and activists in their mosques and community centres. One police officer said:

Never mind the 'hard to reach', what about identifying groups that understand al Qaida, who represent less than 5 per cent? We should focus more on the community's own counter-terrorism experience and then export this to the authorities, not necessarily the other way around.

In chapter 3 of this report, the question is examined in more detail, with particular reference to Salafi Muslims.

Fourth, the government has been widely accused of setting the entire agenda for PET before the process had even begun. Many of the people we interviewed who had been involved expressed concerns about the government's handling of the process. At a Home Office sponsored workshop in Leicester in June 2006, the event's chairman criticised the department for dictating the workshop's title: 'Islamophobia and Extremism'. His organisation had raised concerns because of hostility towards the title from the community, but he was told that it would have to hold because it was in line with the department's approach. This kind of practice does not promote local engagement; it reinforces the perception that the government is interested only in talking and leading, not listening or partnering. Unsurprisingly, it is having a negative impact on the government's reputation in the eyes of many Muslim communities.

Finally, there has been very little follow through on the proposals generated by the working groups, and many of those involved confided that there seemed to be a 'certain amount of inevitability' about which issues were eventually picked up by the government. A number of those who were involved from outside the Westminster village said that they felt that their involvement was little more than a government legitimation exercise: their role was to rubber-stamp a process over which they had little or no control.

The most serious impacts, though, are those being felt *within* Muslim communities. Many Muslim leaders had to ask their communities to make a leap of faith. They took personal risks by actively persuading the sceptics among them to participate in PET, and, following the hollowness of the exercise, many feel they wasted their hard-earned legitimacy and have undermined their standing within their communities. Anecdotally, some Muslims are beginning to shun government-run events; one woman told us: 'I was thinking of going along to that event, but I found out it's being run by the Home Office, so there's no way I'm going.'

The government received similar criticism for its later handling of the consultation on legislation to give the police new powers to deal with extremism in cooperation with communities, particularly in places of worship. The paper emphasised that this was a subject on which communities themselves had asked for support,[20] a claim which the Muslim Council of Britain (MCB) has denied. Iqbal

Sacranie stressed that the vast majority of people consulted by his organisation 'rejected the impression that the proposed new powers are being put forward in response to demands or requests from the Muslim community itself. . . . There was never any such demand or request.' Criticisms did not just come from the community: Rob Beckley of the Association of Chief Police Officers (ACPO) argued that existing powers were sufficient to enable the police to take any necessary action, that the focus specifically on places of worship was 'unhelpful' and that there would 'be a significant adverse impact in many faith communities, particularly the Muslim community'. In short, the proposed powers would 'contribute to current anger about counterterrorism powers and their use by the police'.[21]

One of the reasons that the government is getting things wrong is because it has a shallow and partial understanding of the communities with which it needs to engage, which makes it behave schizophrenically.

On the one hand 'communities' are the stuff of multicultural Britain – they are benign exotic groups that add a cultural *je ne sais quoi* to the UK. The priority for policy-makers is not necessarily to understand the differences, but to celebrate them. On the other hand, in policing and counter-terrorism terms communities represent highly political forms of mobilisation that need to be policed, kept in check or coerced into new behavioural norms. This characterisation of communities as being either passive and benign or active and malign means the government has a tendency to avoid engaging positively with those parts of the community that could offer the most potential in tackling extremism and means that it has difficulty interpreting political, social and cultural signs within the community that could have an important impact on our understanding of the threat and effectiveness of government responses.

Engaging with communities in implementing policy: policing and intelligence

The police are the most visible manifestation of the government's counter-terrorism policies so it is critical that their work does not unintentionally alienate Muslim communities. The Home Affairs Select Committee found in March 2005 that although there had been significant efforts to overcome the institutional racism condemned by the Stephen Lawrence inquiry in 1999, there was still reason for serious concern about the 'continuing gaps between the police and minority communities in their perceptions of police work'.[22] A witness at the Met Police's 'Together Against Terror?' conference said: 'One of the biggest dangers of counter-terrorism policing must be that it will grow the very terrorism which it seeks to defeat.'[23] This is more likely to occur if communities feel that they are being unfairly targeted by the police. As Chief Superintendent Ali Dizaei, a senior Muslim officer in the Metropolitan Police, put it: 'To increase the trust and confidence shown to the police in communities that are diverse in make-up means reassuring these communities that the delivery of police services is fair and untainted.'[24]

An ACPO report published in March 2006 argued for a review to identify ways of ensuring that communities are actively involved in the development of a relatively small number of key operational policies that have a significant impact on community confidence.[25] Three of the most contentious areas of police action are stop and search, the use of intelligence and anti-terrorist interventions.

Under Section 44 of the Terrorism Act 2000 police have the power to stop and search within a specific geographical area in an attempt to disrupt terrorist activity. There has been criticism of the practice, which many argue is counterproductive. Ray Powell, President of the National Black Police Officers' Association, claimed in 2004 that the service was in denial about the disproportionate use of stop and search powers in black and other minority ethnic communities, and argued that there was 'without a doubt a correlation between use of stop and search, confidence within black and ethnic minority communities, and recruitment to the police from these communities'.[26] Chief Superintendent Ali Dizaei of the Metropolitan Police has also argued that use of stop and search is hindering the flow of community intelligence: 'Community intelligence should tell us about the people acting oddly, and stop and search is stopping this. We need that community intelligence to deal with terrorism and street crime in our areas.'[27] Almost all of the Muslims we spoke to had either been stopped themselves, or knew of a relative or friend who had been. Experience tells us that this kind of low-level everyday 'humiliation' can have a damaging impact on communities and makes them less able and inclined to cooperate with the authorities.[28]

Pragmatists tell us that Muslims should accept minor inconveniences for the greater good of national security, and that the police should focus their efforts on those who fit the 'profile' of an 'Islamic' terrorist. The Chief Constable of the British Transport Police (BTP), Ian Johnston, for example, has said: 'We should not waste time searching old white ladies. It is going to be disproportionate. It is going to be young men, not exclusively, but it may be disproportionate when it comes to ethnic groups.'[29] His proposals have been met by a cool reception not only among Muslims, but within the police, too. This is not just because there is a growing recognition of the harm this approach can do to community relations, but because there is no evidence to suggest it is effective in disrupting attacks.

The police are aware of the potential damage that can be caused by stop and search. Many forces have developed initiatives whereby officers go into local schools with predominantly minority ethnic pupils to explain the rationale for the procedure, the rights of those being stopped, and to show that the numbers of minority ethnic people stopped and searched are a reflection of the town's demography, not of police prejudice. Chief Superintendent David Baines, who was responsible for implementing the recommendations of the Ritchie Report into the racial disturbances in Oldham in May 2001 has cited the importance of such visits in providing information to replace perception with fact.[30]

Events such as the wrongful shooting of Jean Charles de Menezes and the Forest Gate raid, alongside the growing number of suspects detained under anti-terrorism legislation before being released without charge, cause many – Muslims and non-Muslims – to question the soundness of police intelligence. One woman said:

> When we hear about things like the shooting of that totally innocent man on the tube, or the raid of the house in Forest Gate, it makes us scared. I thought the police were supposed to be there to keep us safe – it doesn't feel like that, though.

A young person said:

> Sometimes it makes me want to laugh, sometimes cry. When you hear about these things it makes you think they really don't know what they're doing. But that also scares me a lot, too.

There have been growing calls for some kind of independent scrutiny for police intelligence. On 17 June 2006, the police announced that proposals to allow a certain amount of private assessment would be considered as part of the internal review of the Forest Gate operation. Chief Constable Matthew Baggott, ACPO's lead on race and diversity, said:

> The issue of public confidence in the police is such that if you could have some degree of confidential, independent assessment that did not undermine the fundamental human rights of the sources and other issues of grave operational importance we would be open to that and support that.[31]

Azad Ali, chair of the Muslim Safety Forum, told us: 'I appreciate that this kind of openness will be difficult, but it's a critical step towards building trust within the Muslim community and improving the quality of our counter-terrorism policing.'[32] As we outline later on in this report, there are existing models of intelligence-sharing that could be adopted for this purpose.

Relations between Muslim communities and the police are put under greatest stress during anti-terrorist interventions, such as raids or arrests. Such incidents rarely endear the individuals involved to the police (or vice versa), but addressing the ways in which they are conducted can limit the ripple effect across the community. ACPO's submission to the Home Affairs Committee in September 2004 described the progress made in this area: all counter-terrorist operations now have a separate community operation order, they have produced a good practice guide in respect of community considerations gathered from counter-terrorist operations; a 'Community Impact Assessment Document and Guidance' has been circulated to forces for use in terrorist operations; a guide to operations in religiously sensitive premises has been produced and circulated to forces; and Muslim contacts have been identified who can provide confidential advice concerning sensitive matters and can be assigned, where appropriate, to operations. But there are still very few Muslim officers trained in specialists operations, which severely limits the Met's ability to make this final recommendation work in practice. A recent initiative by the Metropolitan Police aims to address this (see case study 1).

Case study 1: The Cultural and Communities Resource Unit

The Metropolitan Police's Cultural and Communities Resource Unit (CCRU) was founded in 2003 in the wake of the investigations into the murder of Damilola Taylor and the Soho nail bombing; in these two investigations black and gay officers, respectively, were used to help penetrate the relevant communities, both of which had a traditional suspicion of the police. The unit runs a confidential database of officers who volunteer their expertise in a particular area and officers heading particular investigations or operations can contact the unit to request details of officers with the expertise they require. The CCRU's founding director, Detective Chief Inspector Keith Fraser, told us:

This database allows us to match up the 'life skills' – as well as the professional skills – that officers have with the needs of a particular

---

case. The database contains all sorts of information, not only about an individual's race, ethnicity, faith or cultural experiences, but also things like experience of child abuse, black magic, hostage situations, and so on. It is a really rich resource and allows us to bring new and subtle understandings to our work.[33]

An early example of the success of the unit was when Inspector Steve Biollo, who was in charge of policing the predominantly Algerian community near Finsbury Park Mosque, turned to it for help. The area was home to radical cleric Abu Hamza, and had been the scene of several police anti-terrorism raids; there was a high degree of mistrust of the police among the Algerian community, many of whom did not speak English. The CCRU found Biollo a constable of Egyptian origin from another borough who went to work in the area for two to three days per month, and slowly introduced other officers into the community. Although not Algerian, the constable spoke Arabic and had an understanding of North African politics and culture; as Biollo put it, he 'even went and prayed in the mosque'. The outcome was increased trust of the police among the Algerian community: local people began reporting crimes to the police, and some even made enquiries about joining the police service.[34] The unit was successfully supported by the Muslim Contact Unit (see case study 2), which played a vital role in negotiating the relationship with Finsbury Park Mosque. The success of the unit meant that Fraser soon began to receive enquiries from other police forces around the country, and plans have been made to expand the scheme nationally, although this has not yet happened.

One of the reasons that community relations can become strained is because operations are led by the Anti-Terrorist Branch of the Metropolitan Police, not local police forces. In an interview with the *Observer*, Chief Superintendent Ivor Twydell argued that anti-terrorism raids and arrests that did not subsequently lead to charges created particular problems with the local community: 'People will understandably be concerned when people's lives have been interrupted if there is no obvious, transparent outcome. . . . When the anti-terrorism squad leaves town, we have to deal with the aftermath.' He continued: 'Unless these matters are dealt with carefully, some young people will become radicalised because they believe they need to fight for their culture.'[35] Many Muslims we spoke to made a point of stressing their positive experiences of local police in contrast to their views about national counter-terrorist policing. In London, the Muslim Contact Unit provides a constant point of contact between the local and the national and is able to play a reassuring role when an intervention takes place (see case study 2).

Case study 2: Metropolitan Police Service Muslim Contact Unit

The Metropolitan Police Muslim Contact Unit (MCU) was set up in January 2002 to service the needs of grass roots Muslim community groups tackling the adverse impact of al Qaida-inspired terrorist propaganda at close quarters in London. Typically, partner groups are Salafi or Islamist in complexion, minority sections of London's diverse Muslim population where the seeds of al Qaida ideology had been planted and nurtured over a sustained period often by notable London-based extremists. Given that both 'Salafi' and 'Islamist' had become (and remain) pejorative terms in the hands of leading commentators on what has been dubbed 'Londonistan', such partnership work – between counter-terrorism police and challenging community groups – remains contested. Willing to stand by such community partner groups in the face of criticism, the unit has won respect and trust in the very heart of communities where these vital ingredients have been seriously eroded by a perception that the wider 'war on terror' is often indiscriminate in its impact on Muslim communities (at home and abroad).

While other sections of the Muslim community have sought to tackle the problem of 'home-grown terrorism' merely since 7 July

2005 the MCU has been engaged with expert community groups who recognised at the end of 2001 that Richard Reid the would-be shoe bomber was an early manifestation of a 'home-grown' problem that they had been witnessing and struggling to combat at the grass roots throughout much of the 1990s. As a result of such close, focused partnership engagement the MCU has been able to empower and facilitate pioneering community activity that seeks to reduce the pool of recruits available to al Qaida-inspired terrorism. During the course of such engagement the MCU has also been able to address community concerns including the stigmatisation of sections of the Muslim community publicly 'associated' with terrorism, incidences of Islamophobia, media coverage of these issues, and civil liberties and policing issues.

Those we consulted during the course of this research rated the value of this unit incredibly highly. Much of the trust that it has been able to build is attributed to the skills and qualities of the individuals working for the unit.

Finally, Operation Comfort (case study 3) provides a good example of how police can work proactively to diffuse tensions before they arise after major incidents.

Case study 3: Operation Comfort

Community tensions are likely to be high immediately after major terrorist incidents and Thames Valley Police's 'Operation Comfort' in Slough, one-third of whose population is drawn from minority ethnic groups, provides a good example of the value of police work to reassure the community at these times. Following the attacks of 11 September 2001 there were rising tensions between Slough's various communities. In response, the police pioneered 'Operation Comfort' as a problem-solving approach to defusing potential racial and religious disorder which actively involved the community in the operation from planning through to deployment.

There were regular meetings between operational commanders and community networks on racist incidents, and representatives of the community from groups such as the Indian Welfare Society, the Pakistani Welfare Association and the Sikh Community Action Network were invited to attend full operational police briefings 'to ensure the style of the operation met the potentially conflicting objects of reassuring the community and deterring trouble-makers'. Subsequently, these community observers were also invited to take to the streets alongside the police 'to witness at first hand the effect officers' presence had on the community'. Police commanders also maintained contact with community observers by mobile phone.

All police officers were encouraged to positively engage as many people as possible and to greet anyone within hailing distance with a smile and a friendly gesture. As Superintendent Brian Langston put it, this was intended to overcome the frequent criticism of officers 'wearing their uniforms on their face'. Moreover, in an unusual innovation, the Thames Valley Black Police Association (of which Langston was the founder and chair) played a special role in providing language skills and high cultural awareness that would help the force to engage various sections of the community in an effort to break down barriers.

The number of Black Police Association officers deployed was only small – a sergeant and six officers – but their presence had a huge impact on the perception of the police by the minority ethnic communities in Slough, and created the impression of 'dozens of officers who look and speak like us'. As a result, there were a large number of recruitment enquiries from members of minority ethnic communities, and the operation reduced hate crime and defused tensions, which meant that visitor numbers and town commerce, which had been adversely affected by the rising tensions, returned to pre-9/11 levels. Langston concluded: 'Community participation in policing is becoming part of the accepted way of working in Slough and is making a significant contribution to improving trust and confidence within our diverse communities.'[36]

The threat from al Qaida has been emerging for the last 15 years, and the UK government – like most western governments – failed to see the significance of events until 11 September 2001. After turning a blind eye to – some might say appeasing – al Qaida for well over a decade, events in New York and Washington were a harsh wake-up call, so it should perhaps have been no surprise that the UK government responded so resolutely, shoulder-to-shoulder with its oldest ally. Then when the threat was, quite literally, brought home in 2005, community engagement raced to the top of the political agenda for the first time since Northern Ireland.

Observers of the government's activities over the last 15 years, but particularly during the last five, may well be suffering from the policy equivalent of sea sickness after watching the government steer its approaches to counter-terrorism from uninterested to paranoid, from the front line to the home front. While fierce critics have accused the government at various times of self-interested appeasement or the proverbial 'lack of bottle', the truth is that few saw the threat coming or could have known how it would develop. What is particularly tricky about al Qaida in policy terms is its negotiation of the global and the local; it has global ambitions and scope but needs to be rooted in local communities for its ideas to gain credence. This, more than anything, confused policy-makers and caused the government to lurch between bold manoeuvres and community engagement over the last five years, with the latter never really being taken too seriously. Our framing of al Qaida as a global force after the September 11 attacks was critical in setting the framework for our response ever since.

This chapter has argued that community engagement must be the cornerstone of our policies to tackle al Qaida. But the government's actions in the last five years mean that effective community engagement will not be easy, and is certainly not a low-risk option. Building meaningful partnerships with Muslim communities will require the government to take their grievances seriously, which could open up difficult discussions and disagreements for the government, not least around foreign policy and the war in Iraq. However, taking a risk on engaging on the thorniest political issues, as well as on the ones on which agreement can more easily be reached, will guarantee the government a far brighter legacy than currently seems possible. Understanding Muslim communities and their grievances is the next crucial piece in the jigsaw of a community-based approach to counter-terrorism.

3. The causes of grievance and mobilisation

Caught up in the rhetoric of a 'global' war on terror it can be easy to forget that terrorism is a social and political phenomenon that requires local roots to take hold. While factors such as foreign policy and the Middle East are important, they will have no traction unless they can be linked to sources of grievance and anger closer to home, such as the poverty and discrimination suffered by the Muslim community in the UK. It is therefore difficult to know with any degree of certainty what has driven a particular individual or group to commit an act of terror. Even prerecorded videos by the perpetrators are not always instructive because people are not always honest, or fully cognisant, of the reasons for their actions. Rather than grasping for a single narrative explanation for terrorism, it is important that policy-makers and practitioners recognise this complexity and develop policies that are broad enough to encompass the full range of issues.

Any community that feels itself to be deprived, victimised or threatened will produce members who express their frustrations in a variety of ways. Some will look for positions of power to address injustices through official channels; some will stand back in apathy or through a sense of powerlessness; and others will take to the streets in vocal protest. Sometimes – but not always – a small minority will resort to violence, from riots and street fighting to terrorism and armed insurgency. Understanding the relationships between each of these expressions is critical in devising policies that will be effective at tackling the threat from al Qaida in the UK.

Distinguishing between 'radicals' and 'violent extremists'

The violent and indiscriminate nature of terrorism can lead us to assume that it must be rooted in insanity. But as experts such as Silke remind us, there is no psychology of terrorism; there is no personality type and terrorists do not suffer from higher levels of mental health problems than the rest of the population.[37] Instead, it is the product of calculation, a considered political act triggered by a set of circumstances and opportunities, which requires us to understand the context within which attacks are perpetrated in order to know why such a decision could appear to be good or 'least worse'. Only then will we be able to construct responses to counter those potential motivations.

Policy-makers are struggling to find a coherent approach to the relationship between violent extremists and the rest of the Muslim community. They are keen to stress that, while community grievances are important, they can never be a justification for terror, as if acknowledging some kind of link might imply that the terrorists have just cause or that the government is in some way complicit (the sore point is clearly Iraq). In reality, we cannot divorce these two sets of motives: local anger inadvertently offers a form of 'legitimacy' to the terrorist cause and, when left unchecked, creates momentum around the activity, despite the fact that the Muslim community is not giving its active consent.

At the same time, the government's tendency to hold the whole of the Muslim community accountable for the actions of the few – within an already tense climate of Islamophobia and alienation – has had the effect of driving a wedge between the Muslim community and the rest of British society, rather than between the extremists and everyone else. A lazy parlance in which the words 'extremist' and 'radical' have become interchangeable has meant that any Muslim expressing anything other than unremitting support for the government is under suspicion. Not only does this close down the space for important debates about issues which are causing understandable frustration, but it also means that government tends to speak only to those deemed 'moderate' voices or the usual suspects.

Recognising the distinction between radicalisation (community anger and frustration) and violent extremism is critical, not least because it helps us to shift the calculus for mobilisation. We must remember that all action – moderate, angry, very angry and even violent – is the product of reasoning. The best way to address both the angered and alienated groups and the violent tiny minority of young Muslims is to create a different set of opportunity costs: a framework where terrorism pays less and engagement pays more. Too often, the things we do in the name of 'security' alienate the very people we need to engage. As David Fromkin said over 30 years ago:

Terrorism is violence used in order to create fear; but it is aimed at creating fear in order that the fear, in turn, will lead somebody else – not the terrorist – to embark on some quite different program of action that will accomplish whatever it is that the terrorist really desires.[38]

In other words, when a terrorist kills, the goal is not murder itself but something else, such as a police crackdown that will create a rift between government and society that the terrorist can then exploit for revolutionary purpose.[39]

Historical research on mobilisation shows that violence is more closely related to shifts in institutional attitudes than directly to deprivation or other motivational factors. The cycle is one that begins with violence or terrorism, which brings pressure for institutional shifts, which in turn create the conditions for a different type of mobilisation that is more widespread but not necessarily so violent. Governments are thus – as Tocqueville once famously remarked – at their most vulnerable when they seek to mend their ways.

Our counter-terrorism policies should embrace – not fear – the non-violent mobilisation taking place within Muslim communities.

First, because Muslims who want to speak out have a political right to do so and need to be given the space for a peaceful 'right to reply'. Second, because otherwise we miss the opportunity to challenge the prevalent – and false – assumption that there is a slippery slope from political mobilisation to anger and, finally, to violent extremism and terrorism. This is an assumption that is worth challenging because it entirely misses out the fact that while one type of group may trigger activity in another, the two are not intrinsically linked – other than in terms of the opportunities they create for each other.

Finally, this assumption means that we fail to tap into the enormous energy and passion of a whole generation of young Muslims, whose political commitment is in stark contrast to that of the rest of the British public at the moment. A community-based approach to counter-terrorism may be slow in curbing home-grown terrorism, but it will have important consequences in drawing disaffected Muslims back into mainstream discussions about terrorism and giving them a voice within the public realm. It will also create a situation in which mobilisation can be seen for what it is – a form of political participation with which we must contend politically, rather than annihilate.

Bringing about this shift will not be straightforward or easy. The government is understandably sensitive about any suggestion that its own actions have directly or indirectly caused terrorism; it has to speak to both the minority Muslim community and a majority community, which also feels insecure and wants to be reassured that progress is being made; and it often feels it is having to walk on egg shells for a community that is 'ultra-sensitive' and sometimes reluctant to meet it half way. It also finds it genuinely difficult to navigate the Muslim community, which is complex and fragmented. Being able to tell a radical fundamental from a violent radical extremist is a close call, and one that is incredibly risky for the government. Too often, it is easier – and politically shrewder – to stick to what and who it knows rather than take this chance.

It is also difficult for the Muslim community. Those who profess to speak on its behalf often represent only a minority view within the community and some individuals do not help the image of Muslims. There are also those whose interests are best served by separation rather than engagement. Finally, the community's internal problems are heightening its sense of vulnerability.

Poverty

One of the most striking characteristics of the Muslim community in the UK is its poverty; it represents some of the poorest minority ethnic populations in Britain, in particular, Muslims of South East Asian origin (which account for 68 per cent of the total).[40] On the whole, the Muslim community suffers from poor educational attainment, below average occupational achievement, and an unfavourable tenure pattern in housing. Peach has argued that, 'the net effect of the vulnerable circumstances of the Muslim population, taken as a whole is disproportionately concentrated in areas with the highest indices of multiple deprivation'.[41] As we will argue below, this helps to explain the relationship between religion, identity, socioeconomic status and the mobilisation of a growing number of Muslims, especially the young.

Muslim educational attainment is among the lowest in the UK. In 2003/04, almost a third (31 per cent) of Muslims of working age in Great Britain had no qualifications – the highest proportion for any religious group. This figure is highly skewed to those over the age of 50 – 53 per cent of 50–59-year-olds, 65 per cent of 60–64-year-olds, and 73 per cent of 65–74-year-olds have no qualifications,[42] which raises serious questions about the presence of role models for young Muslims.

Muslims are the lowest performing religious group in terms of unemployment and job status. In 2003/04, Muslims had the highest male unemployment rate in Great Britain (14 per cent), over three times the rate for Christian men, and unemployment among Muslim women (14 per cent) was almost four times the rate for Christian women. Unemployment rates were highest among those under 25 years of age for all the religious groups, but Muslims aged 16–24 years had the highest unemployment rates of all. They were twice as likely as Christians of the same age to be unemployed (22 per cent); a massive one-fifth of all Muslim young men are out of work, a figure that is comparable to France and parts of the Middle East, where the link between economic inactivity and negative political protest has been noted. Shockingly, almost one-quarter (23.7 per cent) of Muslims over the age of 16 years have never worked or are classed as long-term unemployed, which compares with a national average of just 3.4 per cent.[43] Muslim and Sikh men are the least likely to be working in managerial or professional occupations, and the most likely to be working in low-skilled jobs; for example, Muslim men are six times more likely than Christians or those with no religion to be taxi drivers.

Muslims suffer from some of the UK's worst living conditions. Muslim households are the most likely to be living in social rented accommodation (that is accommodation rented from the council or a housing association). In 2001, 28 per cent of Muslim households were living in social rented accommodation. They are also the most likely to experience overcrowding (32 per cent), although this might be partly explained by their tendency to have larger households. They are also the most likely to lack central heating (12 per cent).[44]

Deprivation does not directly lead to violent extremism per se, but we would argue that it can act as a fertile terrain for radical mobilisation once violent mobilisation has occurred. It serves as an effective backdrop against which to articulate grievance, especially where the secular state has either vacated the space of community-based delivery, where state agencies have been seen to be biased or inaccessible, or where it is considered to have failed. What makes the current threat so potent is that Muslims experiencing deprivation in the UK do so at a time when they are highly cognisant of the suffering of many of their fellow Muslims around the world and are angry about what they see as their own government's 'war on Islam'.

Many commentators have argued against the deprivation–violence nexus because not all deprived people become radicalised, and in the case of terrorism in the UK, not all radicalised individualised are necessarily deprived. As Peter Bergen has said: 'Throughout recent history, from the Russian anarchists to the Baader–Meinhof gang in the 1970s, terrorism has largely been a bourgeois endeavour.'[45] We could add that Marx never worked a day in his life and that the nineteenth-century Russian populist defenders of the Russian peasantry were mostly university students. But this would betray an astonishing misunderstanding of mobilisation of any kind: mobilisation is not about rich or poor leaders and/or perpetrators. It stands to reason that those most able to mobilise should be the educated strategists.[46] These types of individuals are not above instrumentalising the belief or suffering of others; nor are they immune to a genuine sense of responsibility in the name of a community, on whose behalf they decide to act. As one expert told us: 'The leaders of [violent] organisations may be educated, but [they] are close enough to poverty for these acts to be about solidarity with profoundly disadvantaged communities in the UK and abroad.'

In the context of the 'umma' – the global community of which every Muslim is a part – the link between the suffering and perceived persecution abroad and the lived day-to-day reality of a majority of Muslims from South East Asia seems even more incontrovertible to those who feel personally persecuted in their daily lives and collectively persecuted as a part of their imagined community. This is especially true in an age when satellite television and cheap flights have brought British Muslims – even the poorest – into much closer and more frequent contact with the experiences of their relatives back 'home'. These links, and the resulting sense of perceived persecution, are likely to be most strongly felt by those well informed and educated enough to make the link between the two.

Finally, it is worth reflecting on basic demographics: it is no coincidence that the growth of terrorism in the name of Islam has taken place at a time when the Islamic world is one of the most youthful – including Islamic countries and Muslims living in the West. In the UK, for example, one-third of Muslims are under 16 years of age, compared with one-fifth for the population as a whole. Terrorism is a crime of the young, which tends to occur when the proportion of young people in a given society rises, thereby often creating a sense of dislocation and imbalance between the generations. Most people who join a terrorist group are young (in their teens and early twenties) and male; the average age of new recruits to al Qaida is 25 years and it is generally the younger members who carry out the most violent attacks. These circumstances were last seen in Europe in the postwar period, when the baby boom generation came of age and had entirely different attitudes and expectations from their parents. During this period, a number of European countries experienced terrorism, including the Baader–Meinhof group in Germany, the Red Brigade in Italy, the IRA in Great Britain, and ETA in Spain, and most members of the current cabinet were engaged in what were called 'radical politics'.

Foreign policy

Foreign policy is, without a doubt, one of the most significant sources of anger within the Muslim community in the UK and is contributing to the community's growing sense of alienation. Its ability to provide a connection between personal grievances, conditions in countries of origin and the situation for the rest of the Islamic world make it a particularly potent catalyst for mobilisation. As one person explained:

Foreign policy can alienate people in the same way that socioeconomic conditions can . . . it creates the same sense of solidarity, often regardless of the actual religious practices of the people involved . . . they don't have to be extremely devout Muslims for people to feel the injustice against them very sharply.

A community leader said:

I would expect young people to get angry at what the government is doing – that's what young people do. But I am becoming increasingly alarmed at the number of my friends – people who have so far been pretty much on side – who are now very angry with this country's foreign policy and as a result are becoming more radicalised in their views.

While Muslims have genuine concerns about specific aspects of British foreign policy – Israel–Palestine, Lebanon, Iraq, Afghanistan, Chechnya, Bosnia, and the shadow of colonialism that continues to hang over relations between Britain and the Islamic world – one of the most important problems with foreign policy is the question of *how* foreign policy-making is done. Whereas participation, public engagement and partnership have become central principles in domestic areas of policy-making, foreign policy remains the preserve of a small number of mandarins and policy wonks. It is frustrating enough to feel that foreign policy is working against you as a faith group, but when you have very little access to the decision-making process the sense of helplessness is increased. This has been particularly true since 7 July, when the government was quick to close down any discussions about the relationship between foreign policy and terrorism, especially in relation to the war in Iraq.

Some argue that Britain's foreign policy is one of the most important drivers of home-grown terrorism in the UK. In a recent open letter to the British government, a number of prominent Muslim leaders – including Muslim MPs – called on the government to recognise that its foreign policy is fuelling terrorism; and both Mohammed Siddique Khan and Shehzad Tanweer cited foreign policy as one of their main motivations in their video messages. And this argument was made by most of the Muslims we spoke to during the course of this research project. Salma Yaqoob, for instance was pleasantly blunt:

> *Excuse me but you're sitting here asking me about the causes of terrorism and we're going round the houses examining potential causes – but there's an elephant in the room: the war in Iraq. Look no further.*[47]

We will never know with any certainty the true impact of foreign policy on terrorist activity in the UK. And there are well-known dangers linked to policy change in response to terrorist demands. There are, however, clear links to be made between certain aspects of

Britain's foreign policy, the way in which decisions are made and the increased mobilisation of many British Muslims – young and old, radical and moderate. Attempts to silence these debates are likely to enflame tensions further and close off what could be a positive and fruitful channel for enhancing relationships between the government and the Muslim community. In particular, our discussions with young Muslims were in direct contrast to the prevalent view of apathetic young people that we hear voiced so often in the UK today, and it is vital that the energy of those who feel passionate enough to speak out is positively channelled into the public realm. Although the current Labour government might have 'personal differences' with the Respect Party, many we spoke to acknowledged the important role it is playing in providing a forum for young Muslims to channel their grievances positively.

Islam

Islam is going through a period of transition. As many commentators have argued, what is taking place now in the Muslim world is an internal conflict between Muslims, not an external battle between Islam and the West; a rivalry is raging in Islam over who will write the next chapter of its history.

The roots of the more recent and visible divisions in Islam can be traced back to events in the late nineteenth and early twentieth centuries. As the battle between pan-Islamist and pan-Arabic forces engulfed the wider Middle East, this era saw the emergence of Hasan al-Banna, a young scholar who rejected both schools of religious thinking and who argued instead that the only path to Muslim independence and self-empowerment lay in reconciling modern life with Islamic values, a process he referred to as 'the Islamization of society'. This gave rise to the formation of the Muslim Brotherhood, one of today's most important forces within Islam.

al-Banna was convinced that the state could be reformed only by reforming the self – a highly peaceful and spiritual process. But this approach was not shared by his successors and after al-Banna's assassination in 1949, Sayyid Qutb emerged as the father of Islamic radicalism. Qutb agreed with al-Banna that society's inequalities could be addressed only by asserting the superiority of Islam as a complete social, political and economic system. However, unlike al-Banna, he envisioned that process to be a revolutionary and violent one that could be brought about only through the establishment of an Islamic state.

Qutb's radicalised vision of a political Islam completely transformed the landscape of the Middle East, giving rise to a new ideology of Islamism. It called for the creation of an Islamic state in which the sociopolitical order would be defined solely according to Muslim values.

The current picture emerges with the contemporary influence of modern Wahhabism (an ultraconservative and puritanical ideology that many Muslims refer to as 'fundamental'). Based on the teachings of the eighteenth-century scholar Muhammad Ibn Abd al Wahhab, Wahhabism is said to have influenced al-Banna in his quest for a pure, legal form of Islam, a return to the word and the way of the prophet. Wahhabism was, however, a minor current in Islam until the 1920s and the late 1930s, when the discovery of oil in Arabia allowed its influence to spread across the region, greatly affecting the religiopolitical ideologies of Mawdudi's Islamic Association, Palestinian Hamas and Islamic Jihad, to name only a few groups. A form of Wahhabism rooted in the teachings of al-Banna and the Muslim Brotherhood is thereby defining of an entire region's brand of Islam in opposition to Qutb's version.

This history is important to the current situation for three reasons. First, and simply, because during the first Gulf War in 1991, a small group of Saudi dissidents calling themselves al Qaida took up the original revolutionary ideology of Wahhabism and turned against the Saudi royal family, whom they accused of selling the interests of the Muslim community to foreign powers. Thus Wahhabism is the ideological starting point for al Qaida, although most Wahhabis and Salafis of course see their use of violence as a perversion of their faith.

Second, it is important in reminding us of the complex nature of Muslim communities in the UK. For the non-initiated – and apparently for large chunks of the media – Islam is an imposing, monolithic religion portrayed as increasingly at odds with western values. But quite the opposite is true: there are many Islams, many communities, many sources, and therefore many contenders for the Truth. This has a number of repercussions in faith terms, most of which we need not dwell on here. What should concern us, however, is the consequences of this fragmentation for community organisation and community–government relations. In the search for an easy one-size-fits-all approach the government has done little to tailor its approaches to the various parts of the community and is still feeling its way along. Paying close attention to the divisions within Islam will allow both the government and the security forces to tailor their responses appropriately and see beyond surface appearances to more effectively 'read the signs' within the community.

Finally, this history is important because it explains the attraction of a 'religious' solution to the grievances and frustrations that we have described. Despite the fragmentation of Islam – and in fact perhaps due to the buoyancy of the debate and dynamism imparted by contestation – both Qutb's radical political Islam as well as the specific teachings of Wahhabism and Salafism provide a language, rhetoric, concepts and ideas that can appear to offer an outlet for those angry young men who feel moved to violence. More generally therefore, religion provides, on the one hand, a neat justification for violent acts, a way of packaging anger and hatred to give it a significance beyond the individual's local and personal circumstances (the fact that Qutb and al-Banna fell short of advocating violence gets lost in translation); and on the other hand, stopping short of a justification for violence, a compelling ideology in a world where the opportunities for great ideological vistas and commitments have vanished.

For a growing number of western Muslims, Islam has become a force for social and political mobilisation: religion has a shared value across the community, across generations and across locality and is a highly effective organisational and rhetorical device, as well as being a spiritual guide for their everyday lives, actions and relationships.

When it takes on this specific mobilisational function, religion becomes an ideology, a programme for change which takes beliefs to the level of collective action. In the case of Islam, this is particularly easy to achieve, not because Islam is prone to ideological capture, but because it speaks of day-to-day acts as much as doctrine; in fact the two are inseparable.

Considering the ideological potential of Islam, we can therefore read the mobilisation around it in two ways that are not mutually exclusive. The first is to take Islam's ideological potential and look for what Tarrow refers to as a 'repertoire of contention',[48] a set of values and precepts from which one constructs meaning and mobilises social networks into action. But as pointed out by scholars, these resources come into play only when there are visible incentives for activism[49] (of whatever sort, violent and non-violent).

The second way in which to understand the role of Islam is to view it, as Modood argues, as an identity movement[50] in which religion plays the crucial role of catalyst.

Neither of these interpretations diminishes the commitment of those who use Islam as a guide – they do, however, point to the potential for instrumentalisation and mobilisation inherent to any system of belief, and, in particular, powerfully organised ones such as religions.

The internal conflict within Islam is being played out most acutely within the widening gulf between the older and younger generations. With few formal or informal mechanisms through which to vent their frustrations, the sense of voicelessness among young Muslims is growing. Many of the young people we spoke to described their discontentment at how their communities are run, and the fact that women and young people in particular are denied access to key institutions and decision-making forums. Many contrast the cultural Islam of their parents, with its strict social and cultural norms, with a purer form of Islam that will allow them to reconnect with the texts and interpret them in ways that seem more appropriate for the next generation. Many parents reflected, 'our children know their faith better than we do'.

These issues are especially interesting as they relate to Muslim women, who are turning to Islam for empowerment. One school girl said: 'They just don't want us to be involved. They say it is all part of Islam, but that's not the Islam I know. Most of the mosques in Leicester don't even let women in, so how can we make our voices heard?' And at a seminar in the city on engaging young Muslims, one young woman asked about this point and was told by the imam on the panel that the community was already doing a lot for the women and girls because they provide services such as childcare and women's fun days. This was met by tutting and raised eyebrows by the girls in the back row. The emancipation of Muslim women through their faith contradicts the stereotype of the weak woman, forced to wear a veil by her dogmatic husband. Such views obscure the fact that the most important gender development within these communities is one of demasculinisation, which is of course important to the problem of home-grown terrorism.

While some parts of the Muslim community are becoming more pious, it would be a mistake to assume that there is strong link between this trend and the growth of terrorism in the name of Islam. There is little evidence to suggest that those involved with al Qaida are more religious than the rest of the community; in fact, for many the reverse could be said to be true. Most al Qaida recruits are not highly religious before they make the decision to join the jihad; only 17 per cent received Islamic primary or secondary education and very few came from highly religious families.

Stephen Holmes[51] argues that we are giving too much, rather than too little, attention to religion because we know more about religion – or religiosity – than we do about the complex politics of the Middle East, so are more likely to interpret actions through this lens. He argues that evidence about the individuals involved in the September 11 attacks suggests that they were driven more by narratives of blame, personal problems and dislocation than by Islamic fundamentalism or religious belief.

In conclusion, the crisis within Islam and today's violent extremism against the West can ultimately be explained only through an understanding of the impact of the colonial legacy on relations between the Islamic world and the West. It was during the colonial period that the strain of Islam was born that would go on to lend its language and rhetoric to al Qaida, and it is the colonial legacy which helps to join up, and make sense of, the links between the situation of Muslims in the West, whose parents and grandparents lived through this important period in history and the experiences of Muslims living in the Muslim world today.

Ties that bind

It is impossible to talk generically about 'the' Muslim community. In reality, it is a 'group' of around two million people whose values, experiences and ways of life vary enormously according to a number of factors, such as age, gender, religious practice, political position and socioeconomic standing. Perhaps one of the most important factors in relation to the positive and negative mobilisation of Muslim communities in the UK is ethnicity. As Humayun Ansari wrote: 'Behind the appearance of religious homogeneity, Muslims in Britain are distributed into ethnically distinct communities upholding a broad range of sectarian allegiances.'[52] Ties to the immigrants' home countries and political developments taking place there are key to understanding both the political processes taking place in the UK and the diversity of Muslim communities, and this means that policy-makers need to expand their field of focus to factor in developments in home countries, and consider the use of interventions there, as well as in the UK.

In an article written for OpenDemocracy, for example, Delwar Hussain traces the radical islamisation of the Bangladeshi community in east London to events in Bangladesh.[53] In this strikingly brave piece, he examines the rise of the influence of the Jamaat Party in Bangladesh and what he calls 'its attempts to revive religion as an instrument to redefine national identity'. Hussain's depiction of how these conflicts both endure and are transformed in the context of London's neighbourhood of Tower Hamlets via a number of local organisations illustrates the delicate interplay between local conditions (the politics of Tower Hamlets) and power struggles imported from abroad:

> In Bangladesh, secularists and the left have been marginalised and suppressed by the post-2001 ruling coalition. While the Bangladesh Nationalist Party – and George Galloway in London – seek to ride the Jamaat-e-Islami tiger for political gain, the prospects of this strategy for resolving the enduring questions of social justice, equality and diversity are dim.[54]

Similar powerful ties between the Kashmiri communities and Azad Kashmir exist. Like other South Asian communities, the Kashmiri social structure is based on the extended family, but the wider kinship network of 'biraderi' ('brotherhood' loosely translated) is vital to understanding the way that Kashmiri diaspora communities behave, how they mobilise and how they relate to what is happening 'back home'.

Biraderi allows individuals to trace common ancestors and patrilineage, thus providing its members with a sense of security and self-assurance. Since there are a number of biraderis operating within the Azad Kashmiri community in Britain, their level of influence can affect the internal and external relationships of the community as a whole. Biraderi networks in Britain are essentially a reflection of the social organisation of Azad Kashmir and of what happens when this social organisation is transplanted to a different context.

Therefore, as pointed out by Ellis and Khan:

> Kashmiri political activity [in Britain] provides an important and perhaps unique insight into the complexity of ethnic politics in Britain today. The Kashmiris have incorporated political aspirations for their land of origin into their involvement with British politics, and have succeeded in changing 'foreign affairs' into 'home affairs' for British parliamentarians. British politicians have had an involvement with the affairs of Kashmir since the early days of the British Empire. However, the nature and reasons for this interaction have changed over this period.[55]

These kinds of patterns are not new and can be seen in other immigrant groups. The Irish and, perhaps even more so, the Italian communities of the eastern USA in the early twentieth century offer an obvious point of comparison. Consider the displacement of large groups of individuals from the poorer parts of a given country, exhibiting strong family ties and a culture of strict religious belief. These communities arrived in wave after wave, thus ensuring both a strong bond between the country of origin and the country of emigration, as well as the re-enactment and continuation of the political and social strife of the homeland. The situation they faced is not so different from that of the Muslim community in the UK today, and such a comparative outlook should lead to optimism: over time these communities, once demonised, feared and perceived as self-segregating, became among the most successful in their new countries.

These ties to the home country are becoming more and more important. With the advent of satellite television, cheap air fares and the 24/7 global media, even poor and deprived communities are able to maintain very close relationships with their home countries in ways that were not possible even a decade ago. This makes questions of loyalty and identity increasingly complex and means that influence and power can lie far from 'home' and beyond the control of national politicians in the UK.

Therefore policy-makers must think differently about how and where they work. They first need to ensure that they have a sound and sophisticated understanding of regional politics and how this is likely to impact on Muslims living in the UK. This is not an expertise that is normally found outside the Foreign and Commonwealth Office (FCO), so it is increasingly important that the FCO collaborates with domestic government departments to ensure they have the relevant knowledge. Second, policy-makers and practitioners need to reconsider the channels of communication they use. This does not just mean working through Islamic media organisations in the UK, such as the Islam Channel, but might increasingly also mean communicating through satellite television channels from countries such as Pakistan, Bangladesh or Somalia.

Dislocation can leave individuals vulnerable to recruiters. The academic Marc Sageman has argued that social bonds are the critical factor in an individual's choice to join a terrorist group.[56] Formal affiliation with the jihad seems to be a group activity, with friends deciding to join as a group rather than individually; in 68 per cent of cases friendship ties and pre-existing relationships are important factors in the recruitment of an individual to al Qaida. The formation of a strong friendship group also creates a sense of one-upmanship among the friends, which motivates closer and more practical involvement. This is not specific to al Qaida. Wasmund talked about 'total groups' in relation to the German Red Army Faction: they were intense, tightly knit social groups that satisfied their members' social, emotional and spiritual needs.[57]

Dislocation is not unique to Muslim or even all minority communities; in the UK, social networks and family patterns have been disrupted following rapid social change brought about by forces such as urbanisation, globalisation and increased flows of people between countries. In many ways, it is this social dislocation that is fuelling the government's sometimes heavy-handed response, which then reinforces the sense of isolation among Muslims and fear within the rest of society. The priority for policy-makers and politicians should be to break this cycle to create the space for more progressive responses to terrorism to develop. We need an effective community-based approach to counter-terrorism.

4. Putting communities at the heart of counter-terrorism

Bringing it Home argues that we need to put communities at the heart of our approaches to counter-terrorism. First, **communities offer important sources of information and intelligence; they are our own in-built early warning system.** This is especially important against a group such as al Qaida, which is willing to inflict mass carnage with no warning whatsoever. Second, **communities picking up these signs are best placed to act pre-emptively to divert their young people from extremism: the self-policing society.** Third, while the state must also play a role, **communities must take the lead in tackling problems that either create grievances or hinder their ability to organise,** such as poverty, poor educational and employment attainment, and the paucity of effective leadership and representation.

Finally, and perhaps most importantly, **the police and Security Service cannot act without the consent of the communities they are there to protect.** There are those who would argue that Muslims should tolerate inconveniences for the greater good, effectively put up and shut up. But this illustrates a lack of understanding about how security is achieved in practice – **security is always delivered through consent, never through force.** The nature of the threat from al Qaida means that the police will often need to intervene much earlier, thereby increasing the risks that they will make mistakes. Sustaining this practice over the long term will be possible only if the police secure the active consent of the Muslim community, which will need to give them the benefit of the doubt on such occasions.

Our research shows that a community-based approach to counter-terrorism must be underpinned by a number of principles. It must be **locally based and recognise and respond to the differences within the Muslim community**, which is far from homogenous. It needs to be **rooted in an understanding of faith**, without which it is easy for government and security forces to misread the signs within the community. The government must **make the policy-making process as transparent and accountable as possible**, opening up decision-making processes and engaging on issues where there is political discontent. Only then will trust be forged between the government and Muslim communities. On a related note, **the government must get over its hang-ups about responding to the grievances of the Muslim community.** In many instances, they are well founded and deserve to be recognised, but in others the government must be more confident about taking the debate out to the communities, rather than sulking in Whitehall.

A community of communities: why the government needs to get local

During the second half of the twentieth century, the community activist Saul Alinsky worked tirelessly to overcome the injustices that stemmed from racial segregation in the USA. He believed that the community was the most effective level at which to effect lasting change;[58] by operating at the level at which people lived their ordinary lives, groups could inculcate the sort of lasting behavioural change that would create the shift that society needed to go through to become fairer. The problem, however, was that operating in these units meant enforcing the very divisions that were themselves part of the problem. By identifying a place-based solution to a place-based problem, the old divisions had the opportunity to become more entrenched.[59]

For the UK's Muslim communities, this problem is made even more complex by the fact that there is a very limited understanding of the idea of 'superdiversity' in the UK. In other words, majority white communities are fairly good at grasping how minority communities differ from the majority, but not nearly so good at understanding how they differ from one another. In the early 1990s, faced with the challenge of dealing with a complex Muslim community, then Home Secretary Michael Howard encouraged the establishment of the Muslim Council of Britain to act as a one-stop-shop for government with Muslims.[60] As we have seen, the Muslim community is far from homogenous. There are a number of different factors – ethnicity, race, class, gender, geography, time of arrival, and so on – that layer over their faith identity in ways that influence how they live their lives, their attitudes towards non-Muslim British society, their educational and employment prospects, and the structure of their communities. **Understanding differences within the Muslim community is critical to designing the types of interventions and structures that will enable all communities to participate in a community-based counter-terrorism strategy without encountering undue negative outcomes.**

Assuming uniformity between all British Muslims has hampered engagement and led politicians on many occasions to make deeply alienating choices about 'representation'. Many of the Muslims we spoke to were frustrated that the government seems to consult the usual suspects and does not make enough effort to work deeper within communities in order to get to the harder-to-reach groups, especially the women and young people who are not represented within the majority of community structures. As long as the engagement process remains so national in approach and continues to favour a simplified account of the Muslim community, many of the messages and initiatives will have little meaning on the ground.

Working at the community level is hard to get right and requires governments to 'let go', which is risky when the wrong choices can have such serious consequences. Community organisations must retain the confidence of the people who are using them. If users feel that an institution they trust to support them in everyday life has a parallel agenda, its credibility is lost and, with it, any possible value that it could deliver to wider public service and security goals. One participant explained:

> It is essential that this aspect of our work does not suddenly get splashed across a front page. We would lose credibility with our members – they would think we were doing it for publicity or personal profile – and it's vital that we don't lose their trust because without it we are powerless to help.

The government and security forces need to get a grip on faith

Faith must play a central role in our responses to home-grown terrorism and the government must work more through faith-based organisations. In part, this is because those articulating violent extremist views are using faith as their justification. As one person put it: 'We have to fight fire with fire. We can't address a problem that is connected with a wrong interpretation of our faith without using our faith to challenge what they say.' Another said: 'The more a Muslim understands their faith, the more peaceful they will be. An empty tin makes the most noise.' In fact, the stories of the 7 July bombers seem to suggest that for some violent extremists, knowledge of their faith was patchy and had often come to them later in life. 'Mohammed Siddique Khan had very little to do with religion when he was growing up,' one interviewee said. 'It has been the same for a number of the other people who've been involved with these groups. They end up getting a religious education as adults, but with politics layered on top.' Faith-based organisations are also important because they are rich in the sort of social ties that are needed to initiate action.

The Radical Middle Way project – a combined effort between FOSIS (Federation of Student Islamic Societies), QNews, Young Muslims Organisation UK and Mahabba United – is an attempt to have a more public conversation about Islam and the different understandings of the faith with high-profile and reputable speakers, such as Hamza Yousef. As one advocate of the idea explained: 'The project aims to create intellectual space to engage on issues that are confusing and challenging to young people.' The events seemed to succeed in reaching a good cross-section of people, with women making up more than half of the audience, and three-quarters aged under 25 years. These kinds of forums are rare within Muslim communities because mosques tend to shy away from politics. Young people, therefore, have very few arenas in which to debate the issues that matter to them.

Of all the schools of Islamic thinking, the Salafi community is the one that creates the most unease, partly because a good number of the religious scholars whose teachings have subsequently been used to justify violence have come from this tradition. This means that organisations advocating violence also advocate other elements of devotional practice that correlate with Salafism, although Salafism itself does not support violence. Many of the Salafis we spoke to felt that the government and police are wary of engaging with them and we came across an instance during our research where someone was 'warned off' having a Salafi Muslim speaker at an event because of concerns about providing airtime for their version of Islam.

The government must greatly enhance its partnership with the Salafi community. It is precisely this complex relationship between Salafism and a violent rhetoric that legitimises terrorism that makes active engagement so important. Salafis, however, do not tend to be heavily involved in politics, which can limit the avenues for contact. They are often active within their local communities, though; Brixton Mosque, for example, provides information and advice to Muslims and non-Muslims in the aftermath of terror attacks and threats. It has also, with care, introduced political topics into its Friday prayers in order to provide religious direction to its members on these issues, a space to air grievances in a safe and positive environment, and scholarly advice about how to respond in a positive – rather than negative – way. Community-level working is one way to ensure that even Muslims who are unlikely to move towards formal engagement, such as Salafis, can be part of the strategy in the future.

Transparency and accountability in policy-making are key

Ensuring that a community-based approach to counter-terrorism works in practice will not be easy because it will be implemented against a highly charged political backdrop, where politicians and officials must make decisions under intense media scrutiny. Given the nature of the threat, it is inevitable that they will make mistakes, and they must be sure they are able to defend themselves in front of a sometimes unforgiving crowd. They will not always have all the answers or be able to release the information on which they have made decisions, and will often rely on the trust and goodwill of the British public. Under these conditions **it is vital that the machinery of decision-making is transparent and that there is clear accountability within government and community governance structures.** We make a number of recommendations below relating to the importance of strong leadership.

The government must respond to the grievances of the Muslim community

In many cases, the Muslim community has perfectly reasonable grievances, many of which contribute directly or indirectly to the threat from al Qaida in the UK. Issues such as poverty and discrimination provide fertile ground for the discontentment on which al Qaida recruiters prey. Many arguments about UK foreign policy – especially regarding Iraq – are cogent. By refusing to engage with them the government is fast losing the trust of the Muslim community, heightening their sense of voicelessness and as a result is conceding the moral high ground in the 'war on terror'. **The government must take more risks and help to create spaces within which these discussions can be had.**

Bringing it Home sets out a six-point strategy for a community-based approach to counter-terrorism.

Enhancing the lives of Muslims

The government has already shown that it understands the importance of building community resilience in the face of violence. Since the Good Friday agreement, money from the European Union and the UK government for Northern Ireland has been directed towards supporting existing community initiatives and building a sound economic base for the communities there. As highlighted in the case study of Ashton Community Centre (case study 4), these organisations were ideally placed to act as a launch pad for community members looking towards wider involvement, while also acting as a buffer between community members and some of the most serious side effects of their social and economic exclusion.

> **Case study 4: Ashton Community Centre, New Lodge, Belfast[61]**
>
> Ashton Community Centre is on New Lodge Road in Belfast which was, before the peace agreement, the road with the largest number of violent deaths. The community that lived nearby was distrustful of statutory services and the police. As well as being alienated from a lot of mainstream public service provision, the community was under acute pressure. It housed many ex-prisoners and, combined with already high unemployment, meant many families were trying to survive on extremely low incomes. Many people lacked the skills they needed to find work, and many were encountering mental and physical side effects of the years of violence they had suffered.
>
> The impetus for setting up the community centre came from within the local area, and its management and staff were almost all drawn from the community. The centre provides a series of different services, including after-school and crèche facilities for childcare, and IT training and internet and skills development for former prisoners. There were also spaces that the community could use for its own purposes, and facilities to tackle the wider consequences of the conflict, particularly mental health issues.

Ashton's progress has not been straightforward, but the sense of ownership that the community had over the project has been critical. Starting to re-build a sustainable sense of community for New Lodge has meant creating organisations and activities around which the whole community can coalesce to start to address its shared challenges. As part of a community with an increasing number of legitimate tools for building its own resilience, residents of New Lodge are now in a position to tackle the pervasive problems affecting the well-being of their community on their own terms.

Community organisations are often particularly effective in helping groups to overcome economic and social disadvantage. In east London, for instance, work carried out by the Bangladeshi community in tackling poverty and discrimination in ethnically sensitive ways has been documented,[62] and the East London Mosque plays a critical role, offering education, a gym, a youth centre and a library, as well as legal advice and other, less formal types of support.[63] Ensuring that the capacity to run and sustain initiatives rests within the community also helps to ensure that the organisations have a lifespan beyond the immediate policy agenda which, in turn, creates a climate of trust between community members and decision-makers. If interviewees are sceptical about the truth of claims that are being made about support, it only serves to affirm the high levels of cynicism that already dominate relationships with government. One woman told us, for instance:

I can't really believe that they expect us to take them seriously now that they are suddenly taking an interest. My community has been this poor for years. Why are we now supposed to be grateful that people have taken an interest, when it's pretty obviously because politicians have been scared into it?

A later section outlines recommendations about strengthening these community organisations.

While it is true that many of the most effective and lasting solutions to socioeconomic disadvantage happen at the community level, it is important to ensure that this work is underpinned by a national strategy to improve the living conditions and opportunities of Muslims in the UK. **The government should conduct a cross-cutting review of policies designed to tackle deprivation in order to determine which interventions are most effective in reaching poor Muslims,** and the lessons from this review should be applied more widely across public services. In particular, the government must address the poor educational attainment of young Muslims, partly through paying attention to what happens in the classroom, but also by enhancing auxiliary services available to them. Specifically, as part of the ongoing process of change and development in the national youth service, including Connexions and statutory youth services, **the government should increase the involvement of voluntary and community provision that is often better placed to tailor responses to the needs of minority communities.**

Prejudice against Muslims is on the increase all over the UK. One woman told researchers how she had been attacked on a bus after the September 11 attacks. She explained:

> *He called me a f**king Paki, but I said to him that I was from [our town]. In the end, he apologised. Everyone clapped when he got off the bus, but none of them spoke up to help me when he first started having a go.*

Another incident involved two women having their headscarves forcibly removed by a bus driver.

While the government must continue to pursue discrimination through the judicial service, community-led initiatives are effective because they can tackle incidents when they occur, build the types of community resilience that are essential to long-term solutions, break down stereotypes, and build relationships. As David Miliband said when he was minister for communities and local government: 'We need more than legislation, vital though that is. We need to . . . build up the institutions, activities and outlooks that are the bridges between communities.'[64]

In the past, community organisations have inaugurated public celebrations of minority identities which help to counter the negative messages and equip young members of the community with the knowledge to counter criticism from others. On a national level, events such as Black History Month, Race in the Media Awards, the Jameel Gallery at the Victoria and Albert Museum and Islam Expo counter ignorance among the majority white people and the government should step up its support for these kinds of initiatives. Local organisations, such as the Shadinata Trust in east London, also work to raise the profile of the positive aspects of cultural heritage, and deserve more funding and support in kind from local authorities.[65]

Breaking down stereotypes and learning to negotiate difference are skills that are becoming more important to all our young people and need to be developed as early as possible. Although we should avoid the temptation to overload teachers with responsibility for more and more things, there are a number of ways in which schools could play a vital role. Creating environments that value and teach positive ways of dealing with difference and dissent is vital; dissent is a normal part of growing up but for young Muslims it is a particular issue. **The Department for Education and Skills (DfES) should launch a programme of training for teachers in facilitating these types of discussions**, drawing on existing material from countries such as South Africa. Schools should also **prioritise citizenship teaching that incorporates an important element of media analysis to equip the next generation of young Muslims and non-Muslims to question and challenge media stereotypes** about different groups. Finally, the **DfES should establish a national partnership scheme between secondary schools and local media** to give young people an insight into the inner workings of the media, and help them to understand that they have the ability to influence the news agenda.

Strengthening community infrastructure

Research shows that communities with a strong and rich infra-structure are more resilient and better equipped to deal with internal problems. They also find it much easier to engage with the government and others outside their community because they have a ready-made network through which to work. Some Muslim communities lack this infrastructure or have community organisations that are dominated by a small group of leaders, who are reluctant to share power or adapt institutions to the needs of the wider community. Where this is the case, **government and civil society should endeavour to work together to build a more varied and resilient infrastructure**, reinforcing the existing bonds within the community and building new ones between the community and other actors.

One of the most obvious ways that the government could influence behaviour is through conditionality. **Public funding should be made conditional on the extent to which the governance mechanisms of an organisation are reflective of both the technical and professional expertise needed. Government should strengthen its support to organisations that already demonstrate good practice. When it comes to building effective policy, government must talk to as many people as possible. However, when it comes to endorsing organisa-tions by granting high-profile political access those organisations that have passed the representative governance test should be privileged over those that have not.**

Knowledge sharing between community organisations is an important part of increasing community resilience. One way to do this would be to encourage organisational 'planting', when an established community organisation from one place uses its own experiences to support and advise newer ones elsewhere. This mentoring approach has worked with schools and local authorities and – in the case of Neighbourly Action Southall – has been applied successfully with community groups, as well as with larger voluntary organisations. To ensure this transfer happens at the national as well as the local level and includes the smallest as well as the largest organisations, **the Department for Communities and Local Government (DCLG) via Futurebuilders should create a UK-wide network of Muslim community organisations. The focus of this network should be horizontal capacity-building rather than lobbying and representation.**

In some cases, Muslim community organisations, like all others, will not be able to accept state funding because of the need to maintain absolute independence in the eyes of their clients and users. So government needs to ensure that there are strategies in place to allow these groups to thrive outside the realm of statutory funding.

Non-statutory funding organisations are obviously part of the answer here; many major trusts have been seeking opportunities to build infrastructure for many years, including the Barrow Cadbury Trust and City Parochial Foundation. Others are moving in this direction; the Joseph Rowntree Foundation has, for instance, started funding projects in Bradford, as well as York, to incorporate an area with a more diverse community. Other trusts should draw on the expertise of those already involved with funding minority ethnic communities, and **the trust sector should create an informal working group to share examples of good practice and ensure that they are not duplicating efforts.**

For small community groups, good governance must also be a priority. **Management committees within Muslim organisations – just as in other communities – need to reflect the characteristics of people using their services**, as well as having the skills needed to keep within the regulatory framework. So often, women and young people find it difficult to gain access to these forums of decision-making, which means their voices are not heard. Committee members should act as a bridge between their own organisation and others, ensuring that even when groups aren't accessing statutory money, they are still able to link into wider services. **Local government officers should be encouraged to volunteer on management committees, to improve their understanding of the work that these groups do and act as a known point of contact between the organisation and individuals** interested in getting involved with it. Local authorities can support their officers taking part in this sort of work by giving time off for governance duties or explicitly recognising the value of being involved in these activities for career progression.

Improving leadership

Clear political leadership is critical and we recommend three ways in which the government could improve its approach. First, it must take the argument for community-based counter-terrorism out to the public and stand up for this approach in the face of criticism. **The Labour Party should make a community-based approach to counter-terrorism a central agenda item for the policy seminars it will be holding in early 2007 in place of its Spring Conference.** The party should also place a high priority on ensuring that these meetings attract a richer mix of Muslims. The other two main political parties should look for similar opportunities to have this debate, too.

Second, **the government must create a cabinet-level minister with overall responsibility for the whole of the counter-terrorism portfolio**, as set out in this report. While distributed responsibility has a certain logic, the lack of a single point of authority means there is a danger that the 'softer' elements of the CONTEST strategy are overlooked. The new minister for counter-terrorism should be responsible for ensuring this does not happen, and should be given powers of influence across all the necessary departments.

Third, this individual must **ensure that the 'prevent' agenda acquires an appropriate share of counter-terrorism funding during the review of CONTEST, as part of the government's Comprehensive Spending Review.** There are currently no figures available about the breakdown of funding for each of the four strands of CONTEST, but our research suggests that the 'prevent' agenda is the poor relative within the group. The government must address this and pledge to **publish a breakdown on spending of each strand annually.**

Local authorities and Muslim communities need to work together to identify and address the enduring barriers that stand in the way of developing good community infrastructure within Muslim areas. This may necessitate the involvement of an external organisation; in Oldham, for instance, the Institute for Community Cohesion was invited to review the authority's progress after several years of working towards improving relationships between diverse groups living in the town. Other areas may feel that they understand the underlying problems, but need outside mediation support to help to find shared solutions. Local authorities should invite external organisations, such as the Institute for Community Cohesion, to conduct similar reviews every three to five years.

Most importantly, government and local authorities must support the creation of a generation of young Muslim leaders who are ready to take on leadership roles within their own communities and beyond. Partly, this involves demystifying the role played by larger state institutions, with greater openness and transparency where possible, and opportunities to meet and talk to people working in those organisations. **The government should launch a national shadowing scheme for young Muslims to enable them to get an insight into the work of key people, such as MPs, local councillors, journalists and think tanks.**

It will also mean building specific opportunities to equip young people from all parts of the Muslim community – including those with views seen as radical – to take part in activities and networks which will build leadership skills that they can use in the future. The importance of leaders with the capacity to work towards non-violent solutions to serious tensions has been recognised at an international level by organisations such as Seeds of Peace, a group which educates both Israeli and Palestinian young people through a range of initiatives. **We recommend that the government supports a tailored version of the Common Purpose Navigator Programme for young Muslims.** This would provide mentoring, networking opportunities and personal development services that help to develop these types of leadership skills. It could be built up and run through existing school careers services, including those at Islamic schools, in both public and private sectors.

It is also vital that young Muslims have the chance to speak for themselves and contribute to public debates that have a bearing on their communities. To do this, the government should support the **creation of a British Muslim Youth Congress to provide a forum within which young Muslims can discuss the future of their communities and practise the skills of debating and decision-making.** If supported by the community itself, the Congress would, in time, become the voice of young Muslims, making recommendations to the government and community representative organisations, such as the MCB, and provide a platform for showcasing the talents and achievements of the Muslim community. Alongside government funding, it could also seek to attract financial support from Muslim businesses, or businesses based in areas with high Muslim populations, and trust funds.

This report identifies the generational divide as being a critical inhibiting factor to progress in this area of policy. Although **finding authentic spaces for intergenerational exchange** is incredibly difficult, this is something that government, local authorities and Muslim communities must prioritise. This might include activities such as mentoring schemes, social and cultural activities, political debates and increased interface between school and other community-based organisations.

Creating spaces for these kinds of debate will take time because, as a society, we are becoming more and more uncomfortable with expressions of dissent; political parties are concerned to present a united front to the media and electorate, and there are fewer places where we have the chance to argue through key issues without lurching to polemical and often emotionally charged positions. Debate is also difficult within the Muslim community, which has been reluctant to air its internal divides in public, and where there is a long tradition of civility and deference. Unless we improve our track record on handling a plurality of opinions in an honest and open way, people will continue to feel that being enraged by a political decision with which you disagree is a subversive activity in and of itself.

Opening up the foreign policy-making process

Foreign policy is one of the key drivers for frustration among the Muslim community and is often cited as a catalyst or justification for violent extremism by those involved in terrorism.[66] During the summer of 2006, key Muslim public figures wrote an open letter to the government, highlighting the fact that the UK's foreign policy fans the flames of violent extremism and has made recruiters' jobs far easier.

Leaving aside the specifics of situations such as Iraq, Iran, Afghanistan, Chechnya, Lebanon or the Israel–Palestine conflict, the question of UK foreign policy in relation to the Muslim world highlights a wider point about the government's engagement on questions around foreign policy in general. In most other areas of policy-making, the government has come to realise that it might not always be the expert, that non-expert, non-political perspectives are central to identifying effective solutions to these serious challenges, which for many Muslims are intimately linked to their local everyday experiences because of family connections back 'home'.

The last few years have served to illustrate the fact that foreign policy choices are not mechanistic and value-neutral, but are expressions of a government's and a nation's priorities. When decisions are made that do not have the backing of the nation this can cause tension within certain communities, depending on the issues in question. This is especially true when those communities that disagree have not been engaged in the decision-making process.

The government must open up discussions about foreign policy to those outside the Westminster bubble, drawing on lessons from other areas of policy, such as public services, and **learning from countries, such as Canada, which have developed a model of public engagement on foreign policy**. In doing this, it should prioritise debate around the more contentious areas of policy, such as Iraq and the Israel–Palestine conflict, rather than shying away from them. **The Foreign Office, the Department for International Development (DfID) and the Ministry of Defence (MoD) should increase the**

number of staff dedicated to 'outreach' with minority communities in the UK and organise regular public discussions around the country to get community input on key foreign policy questions. For example, as the debate about a possible invasion of Iran gathers pace, the Foreign Office should be organising sessions with Iranian diaspora communities across the UK to gather their perspectives.

Opening up debates about foreign policy would not be merely an exercise in good public relations, but could generate enormous value for the foreign policy machine. Given the interconnectedness of home and abroad and the tight links between Muslim communities and their countries of origin, **British Muslims could provide vital insight and expertise, which would help the government to formulate effective policies. This resource is rarely tapped at the present time.**

Diverting young people from extremism

All young people go through a period of anger and frustration, which is a normal part of the transition from childhood to adulthood, and is especially prevalent among young men and those for whom questions of identity and belonging are problematic. Youth programmes and activities have long been used as a way of channelling these energies in a positive direction and developing key life skills, such as team working, problem-solving, conflict resolution and so on.

Working at the community level can generate alternative forms of activism for young people who would potentially be drawn into violent extremism. Community organisations offer a sense of belonging, in the absence of which membership of violent groups can seem attractive. With social isolation seemingly a key factor for people being drawn into violence, feeling part of a group is crucial. The chairman of Brixton Mosque, Abdul Haqq Baker, knew Zacarius Moussaoui – the so-called twentieth September 11 hijacker who recently stood trial in the US – while he attended the mosque in the early 1990s. When asked in an interview on Radio 4 in April 2006 why he thought Moussaoui had aspired to become a suicide bomber, Abdul Haqq Baker said: 'He wanted a sense of belonging and there was a sense of frustration at the atrocities being committed in the Muslim world.'[67]

Government funding of all after-school youth programmes has decreased in recent years, and in many areas there is an absence of any positive framework for young people outside the classroom. This makes children especially vulnerable to those forces that would promote radicalisation or even violent extremism. **The government must urgently redress this imbalance within all communities, but especially within Muslim ones experiencing extreme poverty, by making available significant funding for community youth projects.** As well as providing activities to keep young people occupied and off the streets, these programmes could also include special counselling and religious support services for those who are particularly vulnerable to recruitment to extremist and terrorist groups, as is outlined in case study 5: 'Street'. This project has the potential to provide all sorts of valuable support and development for young Muslims in London and is a model that should receive state funding and be replicated across the country once the initial monitoring period has finished.

Case study 5: 'Street'

Located in a relevant and informal indoor safe space, this outreach project will provide easy and direct 24-hour access for a significant number of young Muslims in south London, many of whom are regarded by extremist and terrorist groups as recruitment targets. In addition to attractive 'shop front' activities, including computer games, television and leisure activities, specialist support will be on hand to offer 'backroom' counselling and advice in both emergency and routine cases. The project is a proactive Muslim community initiative designed to counter the adverse impact of extremist and terrorist propaganda in a section of the community that is susceptible to it – the Salafi community.

Key indoor activities will include boxing and martial arts training and outdoor pursuits will include white water rafting, mountain walking and camping. Access to legitimate accounts of Islam that challenge the takfiri–jihadis will be available 24/7 on-site and by arrangement with local Islamic centres and local mosques. The project will also receive recently released prisoners who might be vulnerable to recruitment and will establish informal relationships with the local police and specialist units, such as the Metropolitan Police's Muslim Contact Unit.

The project is heavily dependent on the trusted position of the proposed director, Abdul Haqq Baker, currently the chairman of Brixton Mosque, who is a well-known figure within this community. It is a model that could be replicated across the UK, but only in a highly tailored and locally specific way through community figures who are trusted and respected by young Muslims.

Drawing people back from involvement with groups advocating violence must in part draw on religious organisations. One expert explained:

We can only take people on about political theologies if we accept that we have to do that on political and theological grounds. People need to understand the values that are at the heart of Islam. If you take the case of Hizb ut-Tahrir, their views can be critiqued only religiously and politically, not one or the other.

Investment in this work is essential if we are serious about preventing future attacks; incarcerating people will be of limited value unless it is accompanied by active attempts to engage with the reasons for their original offence. 'The most radical young people are on quite loose ground; in fact, even the core can be turned around,' one youth worker said. Community organisations are essential to tackling these issues, someone else explained. 'It is important not to ignore what communities say about these questions, including Salafis. Muslim communities have been fighting against extremism with success for years,' said one participant. One mosque representative argued that 'for mosques, fighting extremism is something we do because it is our moral responsibility, not just because of some sort of political expediency'.

Taking part in this sort of work can make serious demands on community leaders. One person told researchers that 'community leaders have to be very brave . . . there is a general threat from wider society but, also, you can end up facing real and violent threats in relation to work trying to counter extremist rhetoric'. But supporting these leaders is essential. These opportunities to start afresh are critical not only because the best justice systems offer the hope of rehabilitation to all except the tiniest minority of offenders, but also because stepping away from violence is attractive only if people can be offered a real alternative. **The government must put more funding into schemes that seek to pull young Muslims away from the danger of recruiters and those that peddle extremist rhetoric.** But they must be prepared to let these organisations get on with this important work on their own. As one police officer working in the field said: 'Street cred is everything.' This is, of course, risky for governments because there is always a danger that a youth worker will misjudge someone's intentions, or that the government will back an organisation that becomes infiltrated by extremists. But with clear and strong political leadership, this is an issue the government should be prepared to support publicly.

Prisons are also potential focal points for recruitment. People committed to al Qaida ideologies in prison focus their attention on young people held for petty offences, many of whom have very limited religious or political knowledge. As one community leader suggested: 'Many prison converts aren't converts for the right reasons . . . we need to defend the faith against those who misuse it.' To tackle this problem, prisoners need to be offered real alternatives to involvement with extremist groups, which in part relates to offering serious religious alternatives. **The government should increase funding for prison imams and ensure that vulnerable prisoners have greater support after their release**, especially when cultural factors make reintegration into the community harder.

It is crucial that government does not shy away from those parts of the Muslim community whose ideology and rhetoric sit uncomfortably in western secular societies, such as Salafi ultra-conservative communities that hold views that jar with secular liberal societies such as the UK. Part of the reason government doesn't engage with them is because it finds it difficult to distinguish the dangerous from the merely conservative elements in their midst, making any contact risky. Ironically, it is the ability of the two to coexist that allows Salafi communities to provide effective cover for violent extremists, which therefore makes them so central to any counter-terrorism strategy. **The government should fund initiatives such as 'Street', which work with young Salafi Muslims.**

Putting communities at the heart of counter-terrorism interventions and policing

Trust is at a premium for all public services, but is especially important for those involved with the delivery of security and policing, where trust among Muslims has been low for some time. The interviews we conducted around the country took place soon after the Forest Gate raid, which had clearly created a higher level of anxiety among Muslims and hardened views about the 'discriminate' nature of national counter-terrorism policing.

One of the most important challenges raised by this incident relates to trust and pre-emptive police action. As this report has shown, the nature of the threat – the determination to cause mass casualties without warning – and the paucity of police–community links mean that police need to intervene earlier in an investigation to be sure of successfully interrupting an act of terror. But this inevitably means that they are likely to get things wrong more often than they did in Northern Ireland, for example.

However, this is not a power the police can hold legitimately without the consent of the Muslim community, who will inevitably face more restrictions to their rights and freedoms than anyone else. The evidence does not suggest that the community is currently willing to give the police the slack they need; an ICM poll in June

2006[68] found that more than half of British Muslims (57 per cent) thought that it was wrong for 'the police to act to pre-empt potential terrorist attacks, even if the intelligence, information and warnings may turn out to be wrong', as they did in the case of Forest Gate. Reactionary forces have been quick to condemn the Muslim community for refusing to cooperate with the police. Even speeches by government cabinet ministers, such as John Reid, have come pretty close to this. But the truth, as usual, is not as clear cut as these critics would suggest. Events such as the Forest Gate raid have played into a growing sense of alienation and victimhood among many Muslims, who interpret them against a backdrop of growing Islamophobia and an increasingly vocal minority within their own community that advocates separatism driven by anti-western feelings. The truth is that the vast majority of Muslims do of course feel a sense of responsibility for the safety of their fellow British citizens, but are also genuinely scared for their personal safety because of their suspicions about the intentions of the police.

So we are caught in a vicious cycle of dwindling trust. The police do not have the trust of the Muslim community. This, in part, means they have to intervene earlier because they can't take any risks. And each successive intervention makes the trust they need to be able to intervene later and more effectively even harder to build. And so the trust gap grows. But what this shows is that police–community trust is not fluffy public relations – it is central to operational effectiveness. We must break this cycle.

The police need to start by developing excellent relations with Muslim communities that are entirely unrelated to security or terrorism. The community needs to see the human side of the police force, to value its public service ethos, and begin to believe that they are there primarily to solve the community's problems. Our research shows that Muslim communities tend to differentiate between national and local policing, and this is something on which local police forces can build in line with the new focus on neighbourhood policing. **The police need to put in place measures to ensure community relations stop being seen as the soft option for officers:**

they should be measured on the richness and quality of their networks within local communities, they should receive annual feedback from the communities within their area, and good community relations performance should become a requirement for promotion. Officers need support to be able to realise this vision; there should be **greater access to training about Islam and the political histories of the countries of origin of the residents in their area.**

These initiatives will take time to bear fruit and must not be rushed, but in the meantime, the police and Security Service must continue to deal with the immediate threat we face. However, it should not be 'business as usual' for these agencies. While it is true that the police are unlikely to receive a friendly welcome whenever they raid a house or arrest a suspect, there are ways in which they could adapt their working practices to reduce the sense of collective humiliation felt by the community whenever something like this happens. We learned this lesson through bitter experience in Northern Ireland and it is incredible that we so seldom bring this insight to bear on the current situation.

There are a number of practical recommendations that would help to soften the blow on communities of these types of interventions. **First, the police must implement the recommendation that selected and security-vetted representatives from within communities should receive information and intelligence in the lead up to an intervention.** These individuals would then be available to explain events to the community, answer any questions and act as a conduit for community feedback to the police. With safeguards in place to ensure that the initiative did not fall foul of individuals acting in their own self-interest, such as limited tenure and quota systems, this could help the police to avoid some of the most serious breakdowns in relations that we have seen over the last year or so.

Second, units like the Metropolitan Police's Muslim Contact Unit and the National Community Tension Team are carrying out vital work behind the scenes in the lead up to, during and following an intervention. Their links with the community and the trust and legitimacy they have built up are invaluable resources and deserve much greater recognition. **We recommend that the model of the Muslim Contact Unit should be replicated by other police forces that have significant Muslim populations, and that the National Community Tension Team should receive greater backing and have more authority over the work of local police forces.**

Third, the nature of the contact between the community and the police during the intervention is critical. Initiatives such as the CCRU have illustrated the operational benefits of having officers at the scene who understand the community with which they are dealing. **The CCRU should be rolled out across the country** as soon as possible and there must be a commitment to **training more Muslim police officers in counter-terrorist and specialist operations to increase the likelihood of their involvement in interventions.** It is also critical that the **police address the interface between national and local policing during counter-terrorist operations,** which appears to be a source of tension for communities and local police forces alike. As one woman explained to us:

> *When we had raids around here, the only police we had trouble with were the ones we didn't know who came especially for the raids. We told our police officers that we'd had trouble and they said they would try to make sure it didn't happen again. They knew us well enough to know that we weren't going to be making trouble.*

The Head of Specialist Operations, Assistant Commissioner Andy Hayman, should convene a working group to clarify the role of local police forces during counter-terrorist operations, looking in particular at ways of giving them a clear role and making them more visible to communities before, during and after the operation.

Fourth, the way in which the media reports an operation can have an important bearing on the way in which it is received by the community. The police must be careful to correct mistakes in reporting; for example, the media continually ran with the line that the house at Forest Gate was raided by 250 police officers, which quite rightly was regarded by the community as a disproportionate response. In fact, while 250 officers were involved in the operation overall, no more than a dozen or so would have entered the house, and most of the others would have been engaged in activities to minimise disruption to roads and maintain the safety of the local community. Allowing this story to run and run has played into the sense of collective alienation felt by many Muslims. **The police must also ensure they work through specialist media outlets, including not just those in the UK but those in countries of origin for Muslim communities across the UK.**

The flow of information and intelligence in both directions between the police and the Muslim community is vital for the long-term success of our responses to home-grown terrorism. But expecting this to happen spontaneously, or relying too heavily on the recruitment of informants, will not create the trust and partnerships we are arguing for. For example, one interviewee said:

> *I've collected about seven or eight business cards in the last few months, all from police officers trying to 'tap me up'. In some cases, the same police officer has given me his card more than once. This kind of approach does not fill me with confidence in the police, and it does not say much about their 'community partnerships'.*

We recommend that the police establish an infrastructure for this exchange of information and lead the way in openness and cooperation. One potential model for this is **Project Griffin**, a partnership initially between the Metropolitan and City of London police forces and private security guards working for companies across London. The police organise a weekly 'bridge call', which connects into key link points and then cascades down to the several thousand individuals on the ground. The police have taken risks about the information they have given out, but work on the premise that a certain degree of openness makes them more effective. This also provides an infrastructure for the security guards to feed information back through, which is much more likely to happen when they know that they are being trusted and taken seriously. The model would need to be adapted to the specific needs of the Muslim community, but it has proved successful in gathering and disseminating information over a very large group of people. It has now been adopted by a number of other police forces in the UK and overseas, including the New York Police Department.

Delivering a community-based approach to counter-terrorism will not be easy; the government, police, Security Service and Muslim community all feel tired and weary after more than a year of relentless focus on the threat to the UK from al Qaida. From discussions we have had with all these actors it is obvious that each is – to a greater or lesser extent – retreating back into its own community, scarred by attempts to work in partnership to tackle what is a particularly challenging foe.

Bringing it Home argues that this is not sustainable. Not only is there too much riding on a successful counter-terrorism strategy in security terms, but Muslims are suffering from growing Islamophobia and challenges to their freedom, the police are coming under fire for 'trying to do the right thing' and the government is emerging from this period with its trust ratings in tatters.

Soon after 7 July, Metropolitan Police Commissioner Sir Ian Blair said: 'It is the communities that defeat terrorism, not the police.' It is now time to make good on this aspiration and put communities back at the heart of the fight against terrorism.

5. Conclusion

This pamphlet has argued that communities should be at the heart of all our approaches to security, but are particularly important in tackling the new threat posed by home-grown al Qaida-inspired terrorism. There are no risk-free approaches to tackling terrorism, and ours is no different in that regard. But *Bringing it Home* has argued that without the active engagement of Muslim communities the long-term risks will be much higher.

It has mapped out a practical agenda for change, which is underpinned by four critical principles of engagement:

○ The government must get local and stop trying to engage with 'the Muslim community'. Instead, its policies should respond to the diversity within the community.

○ The government and security agencies need to get to grips with faith. Government must continue funding for initiatives like the Radical Middle Way and step up engagement with groups, such as Salafis, who have traditionally been left out of discussions because of their interpretation of Islam.

○ Transparency and accountability in policy-making should not be seen as an obstacle to security but rather an essential element of it.

○ The government needs to respond to the grievances of the Muslim community – either to accept them or to refute them. In order to do this it must agree that no topics are off-limit and foster safe spaces for discussion.

A community-based approach to counter-terrorism has six main components.

Enhancing the lives of Muslims

The government must work in partnership with Muslim communities to improve their life chances and access to opportunities:

○ The government should conduct a cross-cutting review of policies designed to tackle deprivation in order to determine which interventions are most effective in reaching poor Muslims in UK.

○ As part of the ongoing process of change and development in the national youth service, including Connexions and statutory youth services, the government should increase the involvement of voluntary and community organisations, which are often better placed to tailor their responses to the needs of minority communities.

○ It is vital that we create environments that value and teach positive ways of dealing with difference and dissent; dissent is a normal part of growing up but for young Muslims it is a problematic issue. The DfES should launch a programme of training for teachers in facilitating discussions about difference and conflict, drawing on existing material from countries such as South Africa.

○ Schools should prioritise citizenship teaching that incorporates an important element of media analysis to equip the next generation of young Muslims and non-Muslims to question and challenge media stereotypes about different groups.

o The DfES should establish a national partnership scheme between secondary schools and local media.

Strengthening community infrastructure

The government and civil society must work together to build a more varied and resilient infrastructure within Muslim communities to create channels of engagement and networks of support:

o Public funding should be made conditional on the extent to which the governance mechanisms of an organisation are reflective of both the technical and professional expertise needed for its running and its user group. The government should seek to actively strengthen its support to organisations that already demonstrate good practice in this regard.

o When it comes to building good policy government must talk to as many people as possible. However, when it comes to endorsing organisations by granting high-profile political access those organisations that have passed the representative governance test should be privileged.

o As part of the effort to increase capacity, community organisations – including Muslim community organisations – should share experience and good practice through schemes organised by local bodies. To ensure this transfer happens at national as well as local level and includes the smallest as well as the largest organisation, the DCLG via Futurebuilders should create a UK-wide network of Muslim community organisations. The focus of this network should be horizontal capacity-building rather than lobbying and representation.

o Trust funds should establish an informal working group for those organisations working with minority communities in order to share examples of good practice in grant-making and ensure they are not duplicating their efforts.

○ Management committees for Muslim organisations need to reflect the characteristics of the people using their services.
○ Local authorities should encourage local government officers to volunteer on the management committees of community organisations. In order to facilitate this, they should be given time off for such governance duties or have their value explicitly recognised by, for example, being a part of career progression.

Improving leadership

Effective leadership from both the government and Muslim communities will be critical to the successful implementation of a community-based approach to counter-terrorism:

○ The Labour Party should use its national policy seminars in spring 2007 to take the debate about community-based counter-terrorism out to the country. The two other main parties should conduct similar exercises.
○ The government should create a minister for counter-terrorism at cabinet level, increase spending for the 'prevent' strand of CONTEST, and publish an annual breakdown of CONTEST funding under each strand.
○ Where community relations have been particularly troubled, local decision-makers should be prepared to consider the external evaluation – such as, for example, the work carried out by the Institute for Community Cohesion in Oldham – of specific initiatives that are intended to improve community relations.
○ The government should launch a national shadowing scheme for young Muslims to enable them to gain insight into the work of key people, such as MPs, local councillors, journalists and think tanks.
○ The government should launch a tailored version of the Common Purpose Navigator Programme for young Muslims.

o The government, in firm partnership with key Muslim community organisations, should support the creation of a British Muslim Youth Congress.

o Although finding authentic spaces for intergenerational exchange is incredibly difficult, this is something that government, local authorities and Muslim communities must prioritise. This might include setting up activities such as mentoring schemes, social and cultural activities, political debates and increased interface between school and other community-based organisations.

Opening up the foreign policy-making process

o The Foreign Office should develop a model of public engagement, drawing on examples such as Canada. In doing this it should prioritise debate around the more contentious areas of policy rather than shying away from them.

o The Foreign Office, DfID and MoD should increase the number of their staff dedicated to outreach with minority communities in the UK and organise regular public discussions around the country to get community input on key foreign policy questions.

o Government departments should draw on minority communities as a resource, a source of insight and expertise about Islamic and non-Islamic home countries to help develop more informed and effective policies. An obvious example at the moment would be Iran or Kashmir.

Diverting young people from extremism

o The government must urgently address the lack of funding for after-school youth programmes, especially those that are able to offer special counselling and religious support for young people who are vulnerable to recruitment to extremist or terrorist groups.

○ The government should increase funding for prison imams and ensure that vulnerable prisoners have greater support after their release, especially when it is likely that their community will shun them when they return home.

○ The government should fund initiatives such as 'Street', which work with young Salafi Muslims.

Putting communities at the heart of counter-terrorism interventions and policing

○ It is vital that the police and communities have relationships that extend far beyond the counter-terrorism agenda. Community liaison work should become a precondition of promotion, and the police should develop indicators to judge the richness of an officer's community relationships, partly drawing on feedback from the communities. They should also ensure that officers have a proper understanding of the countries of origin of their communities and that training on Islam is available and prioritised.

○ There needs to be a much more open relationship between the police and Muslim communities, where information is shared not on a 'need to know' basis, but on the assumption that open channels of communication are in everyone's best interests. This kind of relationship does not develop by chance, but needs to be grounded within an initially formal process that facilitates the exchange of information between the two. One step towards this would be the roll-out of the Muslim Safety Forum's request for community access to intelligence and sensitive information; another would be to adapt and replicate the 'Project Griffin' initiative between the police and Muslim communities.

○ There should be more dedicated resources for police liaison with Muslim communities on issues of security and terrorism. Units like the MCU should be established in all areas of high Muslim concentration and the National Community Tension Team should be given greater influence over individual police forces.

o   There is a broad recognition of the value of policing communities or specific incidents with officers who have appropriate experience or contacts. For this reason, the model of the CCRU should be replicated across the country as has been suggested elsewhere but not yet implemented. Rolling this out in practice will require further investment in counter-terrorism training for Muslim officers.

o   Local police tend to have strong and trusting relationships with communities, which could be better utilised during counter-terrorist interventions. Local officers should be more highly visible, alongside their specialist counterparts, during operations, raids and arrests. Assistant Commissioner Andy Hayman should convene a working group to clarify the role of local police forces during counter-terrorist operations.

o   Police forces need to pay more attention to their relationship with the media. In particular, they should work through specialist media channels, both national and international, and systematically monitor media output and correct reporting mistakes, on an ongoing basis, as well as during an intervention.

Notes

1   HM Government, *Countering International Terrorism: The United Kingdom's strategy*, Cm 6888 (Norwich: TSO, July 2006).

2   R Gunaratna, *Inside Al Qaida: Global network of terror* (London: Hurst, 2002).

3   D Fromkin, cited in MS Doran, 'Somebody else's civil war', *Foreign Affairs* 81 (Jan/Feb 2002), available at http://evatt.labor.net.au/publications/papers/76.html (accessed 12 Nov 2006).

4   Doran, 'Somebody else's civil war'.

5   R Cowan, 'Terrorism threat has increased: Met Chief', *Guardian*, 13 Dec 2005.

6   J Reid, 'Security, freedom and the protection of our values', speech at Demos, 9 Aug 2005, available at: www.demos.co.uk/publications/securityfreedomandtheprotectionofourvalues (accessed 13 Nov 2006).

7   EF Kohlmann, *Al-Qaida's Jihad in Europe: The Afghan–Bosnian network* (Oxford: Berg, 2004).

8   Ibid.

9   'Hate Club', *Time*, 5 Nov 2001.

10   Gunaratna, *Inside Al Qaida*.

11   Ibid.

12   M Phillips, *Londonistan: How Britain is creating a terror state within* (London: Gibson Square Books, 2006).

13   M Gove, *Celsius 7/7: How the West's policy of appeasement has provoked yet more fundamentalist terror – and what has to be done now* (London: Weidenfeld & Nicolson, 2006).

14   HM Government, *Countering International Terrorism*.

15   See http://news.bbc.co.uk/1/hi/uk/6135000.stm (accessed 16 Nov 2006).

16   HM Government, *Countering International Terrorism*.

17   House of Commons Home Affairs Committee, *Terrorism and Community Relations*, Volume 1, report together with formal minutes and appendix (Norwich: TSO, 6 April 2005).

18   Ibid.
19   Interview with Andy Hull, 21 Sep 2006.
20   Home Office, 'Preventing Extremism Together: Places of worship consultation',
     6 Oct 2005, see www.homeoffice.gov.uk/documents/cons-prev-extreme/
     (accessed 15 Nov 2006).
21   Home Office, 'Responses to the Preventing Extremism Together: Places of
     worship consultation', 15 Dec 2005, see www.homeoffice.gov.uk/documents/
     cons-prev-extreme/responses-doc?version=1 (accessed 15 Nov 2006).
22   Home Affairs Committee, *Terrorism and Community Relations*, Volume 1.
23   Metropolitan Police Authority, 'Community Engagement to Counter Terrorism
     (1)', (26 Jan 2006), Appendix 1, available at www.mpa.gov.uk/committees/mpa/
     2006/060126/09.htm (accessed 14 Nov 2006).
24   *Jane's Police Review*, 13 Feb 2004.
25   ACPO, *The UK Police Service Response to the Threat Posed by Suicide Terrorism:
     Review by the Association of Chief Police Officers Police Use of Firearms
     Committee* (London: ACPO, Mar 2006).
26   *Jane's Police Review*, 10 Sept 2004.
27   *Jane's Police Review*, 24 Sept 2004.
28   S Elworthy and G Rifkind, *Hearts and Minds* (London: Demos, 2005).
29   MPA, 'Community Engagement to Counter Terrorism (1)'.
30   See http://image.guardian.co.uk/sys-files/Guardian/documents/2001/12/
     11/Oldhamindependentreview.pdf (accessed 14 Nov 2006).
31   See www.publications.parliament.uk/pa/cm200405/cmselect/cmhaff/
     165/16509.htm#n169 (accessed 16 Nov 2006).
32   Interview with Azad Ali, 5 Sep 2006.
33   Interview with Detective Chief Inspector Keith Fraser, 18 Sep 2006.
34   *Jane's Police Review*, 12 Nov 2004.
35   M Bright and M Peters, 'We still feel cheated and segregated', *Observer*, 6 Mar
     2005, available at http://education.guardian.co.uk/faithschools/
     story/0,,1432156,00.html (accessed 13 Nov 2006).
36   *Jane's Police Review*, 1 Nov 2002.
37   A Silke (ed), *Terrorists, Victims and Society: Psychological perspectives on
     terrorism and its consequences* (Chichester: Wiley, 2003).
38   D Fromkin, cited in Doran, 'Somebody else's civil war'.
39   Doran, 'Somebody else's civil war'.
40   See C Peach, 'Muslims in the 2001 Census of England and Wales: gender and
     economic disadvantage', *Ethic and Racial Studies* 29, no 4 (Jul 2006); C Peach,
     'Britain's Muslim population: an overview' in T Abbas (ed), *Muslim Britain:
     Communities under pressure* (London: Zed Books, 2005); Open Society
     Institute, *Muslims in the UK: Policies for engaged citizens* (New York: OSI EU
     Monitoring and Advocacy Program, 2004).
41   Peach, 'Muslims in the 2001 Census of England and Wales'.
42   See www.cre.gov.uk/duty/reia/statistics_census2.html (accessed 13 Nov 2006).
43   Ibid.
44   C Peach, 'Britain's Muslim population: an overview'.

45 P Bergen, 'What were the causes of 9/11?', *Prospect Magazine* (Sep 2006).

46 On the whole, active al Qaida members tend to be much better educated than the average person: over 60 per cent have some form of college education, with most coming from technical faculties, such as science, engineering or computer science. Most are skilled professionals, three-quarters are upper or middle class and they are on the whole more globally oriented and speak more languages than average. Almost three-quarters of al Qaida members are married, in contrast to most terrorists, whose men tend either to remain unmarried and without children or will sever ties with their families when they become engaged in terrorist activities. See M Sageman, *Understanding Terror Networks* (Philadelphia: University of Pennsylvania Press, 2004).

47 Interview with Salma Yaqoob, 30 June 2006.

48 S Tarrow, *Power in Movement: Social movements, collective action and politics* (Cambridge: Cambridge University Press, 1994).

49 Ibid.

50 T Modood, 'Foreword' in Abbas (ed), *Muslim Britain*.

51 S Holmes, 'Al-Qaeda, September 11, 2001' in D Gambetta (ed), *Making Sense of Suicide Missions* (Oxford: Oxford University Press, 2005).

52 H Ansari, 'Muslims in Britain', *Minority Rights Group International* 24, no 3 (2002).

53 D Hussain, 'Bangladeshis in east London: from secular politics to Islam', openDemocracy (7 Jul 2006), available at www.opendemocracy.net/democracy-protest/bangladeshi_3715.jsp (accessed 13 Nov 2006).

54 Ibid.

55 P Ellis and Z Khan, 'Diasporic mobilisation and the Kashmir issue in British politics', *Journal of Ethnic and Migration Studies* 24, no 3 (Jul 1998).

56 Sageman, *Understanding Terror Networks*.

57 K Wasmund, 'The political socialization of west German terrorists' in PH Merkl (ed), *Political Violence and Terror: Motifs and motivations* (Berkeley: University of California Press, 1986).

58 S Alinsky, *Reveille for Radicals* (New York: Vintage Books, 1991).

59 ME Santow, *Saul Alinsky and the Dilemmas of Race in the Post-war City* (Philadelphia, PA: Scholarly Commons, University of Pennsylvania Library, 2000), available at http://repository.upenn.edu/dissertations/AAI9989649/ (accessed 15 Nov 2006).

60 Hussain, 'Bangladeshis in east London'.

61 There is a full case study of the community centre in J Craig and P Skidmore, *Start with People* (London: Demos, 2004).

62 Hussain, 'Bangladeshis in east London'.

63 For more information about the East London Mosque see www.opendemocracy.net/democracy-protest/bangladeshi_3715.jsp (accessed 14 Nov 2006).

64 D Miliband, 'Building a community in a diverse society', Scarman Lecture (31 Jan 2006), available at www.davidmiliband.info/sarchive/speech06_02.htm (accessed 13 Nov 2006).

65   See www.swadhinata.org.uk/bak/ (accessed 15 Nov 2006).
66   P Taylor, 'A reason to hate', *Guardian* G2, 1 Sep 2006.
67   Abdul Haqq Baker interviewed by Nasreen Suleman, *Today Programme*, Radio
      4, 20 Apr 2006.
68   See www.ukpollingreport.co.uk/blog/archives/257 (accessed 16 Nov 2006).

DEMOS – Licence to Publish

THE WORK (AS DEFINED BELOW) IS PROVIDED UNDER THE TERMS OF THIS LICENCE ("LICENCE"). THE WORK IS PROTECTED BY COPYRIGHT AND/OR OTHER APPLICABLE LAW. ANY USE OF THE WORK OTHER THAN AS AUTHORIZED UNDER THIS LICENCE IS PROHIBITED. BY EXERCISING ANY RIGHTS TO THE WORK PROVIDED HERE, YOU ACCEPT AND AGREE TO BE BOUND BY THE TERMS OF THIS LICENCE. DEMOS GRANTS YOU THE RIGHTS CONTAINED HERE IN CONSIDERATION OF YOUR ACCEPTANCE OF SUCH TERMS AND CONDITIONS.

1. **Definitions**
   a **"Collective Work"** means a work, such as a periodical issue, anthology or encyclopedia, in which the Work in its entirety in unmodified form, along with a number of other contributions, constituting separate and independent works in themselves, are assembled into a collective whole. A work that constitutes a Collective Work will not be considered a Derivative Work (as defined below) for the purposes of this Licence.
   b **"Derivative Work"** means a work based upon the Work or upon the Work and other pre-existing works, such as a musical arrangement, dramatization, fictionalization, motion picture version, sound recording, art reproduction, abridgment, condensation, or any other form in which the Work may be recast, transformed, or adapted, except that a work that constitutes a Collective Work or a translation from English into another language will not be considered a Derivative Work for the purpose of this Licence.
   c **"Licensor"** means the individual or entity that offers the Work under the terms of this Licence.
   d **"Original Author"** means the individual or entity who created the Work.
   e **"Work"** means the copyrightable work of authorship offered under the terms of this Licence.
   f **"You"** means an individual or entity exercising rights under this Licence who has not previously violated the terms of this Licence with respect to the Work, or who has received express permission from DEMOS to exercise rights under this Licence despite a previous violation.
2. **Fair Use Rights.** Nothing in this licence is intended to reduce, limit, or restrict any rights arising from fair use, first sale or other limitations on the exclusive rights of the copyright owner under copyright law or other applicable laws.
3. **Licence Grant.** Subject to the terms and conditions of this Licence, Licensor hereby grants You a worldwide, royalty-free, non-exclusive, perpetual (for the duration of the applicable copyright) licence to exercise the rights in the Work as stated below:
   a to reproduce the Work, to incorporate the Work into one or more Collective Works, and to reproduce the Work as incorporated in the Collective Works;
   b to distribute copies or phonorecords of, display publicly, perform publicly, and perform publicly by means of a digital audio transmission the Work including as incorporated in Collective Works;
   The above rights may be exercised in all media and formats whether now known or hereafter devised. The above rights include the right to make such modifications as are technically necessary to exercise the rights in other media and formats. All rights not expressly granted by Licensor are hereby reserved.
4. **Restrictions.** The licence granted in Section 3 above is expressly made subject to and limited by the following restrictions:
   a You may distribute, publicly display, publicly perform, or publicly digitally perform the Work only under the terms of this Licence, and You must include a copy of, or the Uniform Resource Identifier for, this Licence with every copy or phonorecord of the Work You distribute, publicly display, publicly perform, or publicly digitally perform. You may not offer or impose any terms on the Work that alter or restrict the terms of this Licence or the recipients' exercise of the rights granted hereunder. You may not sublicense the Work. You must keep intact all notices that refer to this Licence and to the disclaimer of warranties. You may not distribute, publicly display, publicly perform, or publicly digitally perform the Work with any technological measures that control access or use of the Work in a manner inconsistent with the terms of this Licence Agreement. The above applies to the Work as incorporated in a Collective Work, but this does not require the Collective Work apart from the Work itself to be made subject to the terms of this Licence. If You create a Collective Work, upon notice from any Licencor You must, to the extent practicable, remove from the Collective Work any reference to such Licensor or the Original Author, as requested.
   b You may not exercise any of the rights granted to You in Section 3 above in any manner that is primarily intended for or directed toward commercial advantage or private monetary

Copyright

compensation. The exchange of the Work for other copyrighted works by means of digital file-sharing or otherwise shall not be considered to be intended for or directed toward commercial advantage or private monetary compensation, provided there is no payment of any monetary compensation in connection with the exchange of copyrighted works.

c   If you distribute, publicly display, publicly perform, or publicly digitally perform the Work or any Collective Works, You must keep intact all copyright notices for the Work and give the Original Author credit reasonable to the medium or means You are utilizing by conveying the name (or pseudonym if applicable) of the Original Author if supplied; the title of the Work if supplied. Such credit may be implemented in any reasonable manner; provided, however, that in the case of a Collective Work, at a minimum such credit will appear where any other comparable authorship credit appears and in a manner at least as prominent as such other comparable authorship credit.

5. Representations, Warranties and Disclaimer

a   By offering the Work for public release under this Licence, Licensor represents and warrants that, to the best of Licensor's knowledge after reasonable inquiry:

i   Licensor has secured all rights in the Work necessary to grant the licence rights hereunder and to permit the lawful exercise of the rights granted hereunder without You having any obligation to pay any royalties, compulsory licence fees, residuals or any other payments;

ii   The Work does not infringe the copyright, trademark, publicity rights, common law rights or any other right of any third party or constitute defamation, invasion of privacy or other tortious injury to any third party.

b   EXCEPT AS EXPRESSLY STATED IN THIS LICENCE OR OTHERWISE AGREED IN WRITING OR REQUIRED BY APPLICABLE LAW, THE WORK IS LICENCED ON AN "AS IS" BASIS, WITHOUT WARRANTIES OF ANY KIND, EITHER EXPRESS OR IMPLIED INCLUDING, WITHOUT LIMITATION, ANY WARRANTIES REGARDING THE CONTENTS OR ACCURACY OF THE WORK.

6. Limitation on Liability. EXCEPT TO THE EXTENT REQUIRED BY APPLICABLE LAW, AND EXCEPT FOR DAMAGES ARISING FROM LIABILITY TO A THIRD PARTY RESULTING FROM BREACH OF THE WARRANTIES IN SECTION 5, IN NO EVENT WILL LICENSOR BE LIABLE TO YOU ON ANY LEGAL THEORY FOR ANY SPECIAL, INCIDENTAL, CONSEQUENTIAL, PUNITIVE OR EXEMPLARY DAMAGES ARISING OUT OF THIS LICENCE OR THE USE OF THE WORK, EVEN IF LICENSOR HAS BEEN ADVISED OF THE POSSIBILITY OF SUCH DAMAGES.

7. Termination

a   This Licence and the rights granted hereunder will terminate automatically upon any breach by You of the terms of this Licence. Individuals or entities who have received Collective Works from You under this Licence, however, will not have their licences terminated provided such individuals or entities remain in full compliance with those licences. Sections 1, 2, 5, 6, 7, and 8 will survive any termination of this Licence.

b   Subject to the above terms and conditions, the licence granted here is perpetual (for the duration of the applicable copyright in the Work). Notwithstanding the above, Licensor reserves the right to release the Work under different licence terms or to stop distributing the Work at any time; provided, however that any such election will not serve to withdraw this Licence (or any other licence that has been, or is required to be, granted under the terms of this Licence), and this Licence will continue in full force and effect unless terminated as stated above.

8. Miscellaneous

a   Each time You distribute or publicly digitally perform the Work or a Collective Work, DEMOS offers to the recipient a licence to the Work on the same terms and conditions as the licence granted to You under this Licence.

b   If any provision of this Licence is invalid or unenforceable under applicable law, it shall not affect the validity or enforceability of the remainder of the terms of this Licence, and without further action by the parties to this agreement, such provision shall be reformed to the minimum extent necessary to make such provision valid and enforceable.

c   No term or provision of this Licence shall be deemed waived and no breach consented to unless such waiver or consent shall be in writing and signed by the party to be charged with such waiver or consent.

d   This Licence constitutes the entire agreement between the parties with respect to the Work licensed here. There are no understandings, agreements or representations with respect to the Work not specified here. Licensor shall not be bound by any additional provisions that may appear in any communication from You. This Licence may not be modified without the mutual written agreement of DEMOS and You.